CW01646567

The Garden Book of
Sir Thomas Hanmer

The Garden Book of Sir Thomas Hanmer Bart

Introduction by

Eleanour Sinclair Rohde

Cyngor Sir **Clwyd** County Council
Library & Information Service
This book is number

319

of a limited edition of
600 copies

First published 1933
This edition specially produced
by Cedric Chivers Ltd, Bristol
for
The Library & Information Service
Cyngor Sir **Clwyd** County Council
Mold, Clwyd
1991

ISBN 0 900121 35 1

Printed in Great Britain by
Cromwell Press Ltd, Broughton Gifford, Wilts
Bound by
Cedric Chivers Ltd, Bristol

Sir Thos Hanmer Bart

COOPER

1670

THE GARDEN BOOK OF SIR THOMAS HANMER BART

With an Introduction by
Eleanour Sinclair Rohde

GERALD HOWE
23 Soho Square London

The Garden Book of Sir Thomas Hanmer

Now first printed from the MS volume of 1659

under the care of IVY ELSTOB

With an Introduction by ELEANOUR SINCLAIR ROHDE

The Edition is limited to 900 copies
of which 850 are for sale

At the Press of R. & R. CLARK LTD in Edinburgh
for GERALD HOWE LTD London

Spring 1933

CONTENTS

ILLUSTRATIONS

INTRODUCTION

A SEVENTEENTH-CENTURY gardening manuscript of the first importance is a rare treasure, for that period witnessed the publication of the most remarkable books of garden interest in the English language—the *Paradisus*, *A New Orchard and Garden* by William Lawson (the Izaak Walton of gardening writers), Isaac de Caus's *Wilton Garden*, Ralph Austen's two treatises, John Evelyn's publications, notably *The Compleat Gard'ner*, translated from the original of De la Quintinye (who for forty years was the Director of Louis XIV's kitchen garden), John Rea's *Flora Ceres and Pomona*, Andrew Mollet's *Garden of Pleasure*, and Sir William Temple's *Garden of Epicurus*.

To these must now be added *The Garden Book of Sir Thomas Hanmer*. For the author was one of the most distinguished horticulturists during the middle years of the seventeenth century, a close friend of John Evelyn and John Rea, and probably a personal friend of Charles II. He was evidently also a friend of Lord Lambert, the Parliamentarian general, one of the greatest tulip enthusiasts of Commonwealth days and the only gardener who has achieved the distinction of being portrayed in a pack of playing-cards. Lambert was lord of the manor of Wimbledon, where he had a noted garden. In a pack of playing-cards, published during the Commonwealth, he is depicted on the Eight of Hearts, holding in his right hand a tulip. Beneath is the inscription "Lambert, Kt of ye Golden Tulip". Sir Thomas Hanmer contributed to Lambert's collection one of the finest tulips then grown in England—Agate Hanmer—a tulip he (Sir Thomas) had introduced into this country.[1]

Sir Thomas Hanmer came of a distinguished family, descended from Welsh kings and princes and owners of land in one of the most beautiful parts of the Welsh marches. Sir Thomas de Macclesfield, one of the officers to Edward I,

[1] See pages xxi and 19.

settled at Hanmer, and his younger son, Sir John, who married Hawis of Powis of the family of Gwenwynwyn, is reputed to have been the first to assume the name of Hanmer from the lands he obtained there. In the pedigree made by Lewis Dwn (herald in Queen Elizabeth's reign) he is called Sir John de Hanmer. He is said to have been Constable of Carnarvon Castle under Edward I. His grandson, Sir David, was a distinguished Judge, and in Richard II's reign King's Serjeant. Sir David's wife was Angharad, daughter of Llewellyn Dhu (Black Llewellyn) ap Griffith, ap Yorwerth Voel. Their daughter, Margaret, married Owen Glendower. One of David's sons—Griffin—married Guervila, daughter of Tudor ap Grono, the great-great-grandfather of Henry VII. Sir David's son, John, succeeded, and the latter's third daughter married Richard of Bettisfield. John joined Owen Glendower in his rebellion against Henry IV and he also made an alliance with the French king.

This member of the Hanmer family was the last of the native chieftains to claim princely rank in Wales. He held his own parliament at Machynlleth in 1402 and appointed his own Chancellor. His descendant, John Lord Hanmer, writing in the late nineteenth century, states that the family still held lands which had never been bought or sold. Thomas de Macclesfield, for instance, held a piece of waste land, Cronymoor in Hanmer, by yearly payment of a rose at the Feast of St John the Baptist, and of this property John Lord Hanmer says: "I possess the land and in this year 1874 have built a farm house upon it". Sir Thomas Hanmer's father, Sir John Hanmer, who married Dorothy Trevor of Trevallyn, was M.P. for Flintshire, one of the Council of the Marches and a leader of the Puritan party in Charles I's reign. Had he lived he would undoubtedly have supported the Parliamentarians in the Civil War. His son, who succeeded to the baronetcy in 1624 at the age of twelve, became a page at the court of Charles I, and subsequently held the office of cupbearer; one of his predecessors in this office had been George Villiers, Duke of Buckingham.

Before he came of age Sir Thomas Hanmer married one of Queen Henrietta Maria's Maids of Honour—Elizabeth, daughter of Sir Thomas Baker of Whittingham in Suffolk. She was evidently a reigning beauty, for Sir Kenelm Digby was one of her admirers, and in the Cottington correspondence there is a passage in a letter from Howell to Lord Cottington to the effect that there was "an ill-favoured quarrel between Sir Kenelm Digby and Mr Goring, Mr Jermyn and others at St James's lately about Mistress Baker, the maid of honour, and duels were like to grow out of it but the business was taken up by the Lord Treasurer, my Lord of Dorset and others appointed by the King". In 1638, for reasons which John Lord Hanmer says he is unable to trace, Sir Thomas and his brother John were granted passports to travel abroad for three years, "and to take with them two servants, their trunkes of apparell and other necessaries wth a proviso not to goe to Rome".

On the outbreak of the Civil War in 1642 each of them received a commission in the Royalist army, the "trusty and well beloved Sir Thomas Hanmer" being empowered to levy 200 dragoniers "for the better strengthening" of his part of the country. In 1644, however, Sir Thomas received the King's permission to go abroad again together with his wife, son and daughter. Lady Hanmer died in Paris, and two years later Sir Thomas, on his return to England, married Susan Hervey of Ickworth and settled at Bettisfield, where he spent the rest of his life. There are two portraits of his second wife at Bettisfield, one of her as a child six years old and another as a lady of mature age in a white lace dress with her arm resting on a copy of Gerard's *Herball*. Bettisfield had been the chief abode of the elder branch of the Hanmer family since James I's reign. A property situated amidst beautiful surroundings: "Hanmer with its cup of springs, Bettisfield with its barley fields, Bronington wild and forestal, Tybroughton with its plume of firs, Willington spectatress of the hills, Halghton dweller in the clay".[1]

Sir Thomas devoted his enforced leisure during the Commonwealth to his garden. His position in the horticultural world of the latter half of the seventeenth century may be judged from the dedicatory letter addressed to him in Rea's *Flora Ceres and Pomona*—the most important English book of garden interest published between the Restoration and 1700. In this letter Rea, an expert with forty years' experience,[2] describes the collection of plants in Sir Thomas Hanmer's garden as "incomparable", states that the book was inspired by him, and refers to the "many noble and new Varieties" sent him by Sir Thomas. According to John Lord Hanmer, "Sir Thomas's collections seem to have been given to Rea and used by him in his *Flora* and were not published by himself". Rea's other dedicatory letter is addressed to Charles, Lord Gerard, Baron of Gerards Bromley in the county of Stafford, for whom John Rea designed the garden at Bromley, but as the letter shows, Lord Gerard was not an expert. "You will find it" (this book), says Rea, "able to acquaint you with all the glories of our best Gardens, as also how to instruct your own Gardeners." This letter is signed "your most humble and most devoted Servant". But the whole tone of the dedicatory letter to Sir Thomas Hanmer shows that Rea, himself one of the greatest authorities of that period, regarded Hanmer as far greater than himself, and he signs the dedicatory letter to him "the humblest of your Faithful Servants, John Rea".[3]

[1] See *Memorials of the Family and Parish of Hanmer*, by John Lord Hanmer.

[2] "Fourty years are now completed since first I began to be a Planter."—Letter "To the Reader", *Flora Ceres and Pomona* (1665).

[3] There are also verses addressed to Sir Thomas Hanmer's daughter, "the fair and virtuous Lady, Mistress Trevor Hanmer, now wife to Sir John Warner Knight". "Mistress Trevor", who inherited her father's love of flowers, married Sir John Warner of Parham (Suffolk). Both she and her husband became Roman Catholics, and he became a monk and she a nun.

The dedicatory letter runs thus:

To

The truly Noble and perfect Lover of Ingenuity
Sir Thomas Hanmer, Baronet

HONOURED SIR,

These Papers which have long lain by neglected, are at last made Publick, and now come to present you a rude Draught of a Rustick Garden, Planted with such Flowers and Fruits as will prosper in our cold Countrey; a Subject (I confess) worthy a better Author, and sufficiently celebrated in onely saying, it is agreeable with your Noble inclination: and although my remote Residence, and mean Abilities, could not furnish so many new varieties as are to be found in your own incomparable Collection, nor cloath those inserted in a Dress proportionable to their Native Glories; yet possibly many Lovers, less knowing in this delight, may from the perusal in many particulars not formerly published, receive some Satisfaction, and so stand oblig'd to you for the Benefit, since it was your Goodness that first occasioned the Undertaking; for had not your happy Acquaintance reanimated my drooping endeavours in this delight, and your own free Bounty furnished me with many noble and new Varieties, I had certainly long since grown out of love with my Garden, and consequently spared you the Trouble of this Intrusion, as my self the Pains in penning these proportionable effects of idle hours. Sir, I know your Judgement in things of this nature to be Transcendent, as your Generosity, and Curtesie is Superlative, which makes me hope you will candidly Accept and mildly Censure the confessed Infirmities of him that is

The humblest of your
Faithful Servants
JOHN REA.

Sir Thomas Hanmer was not only a close friend of John Evelyn's, but, as the letters quoted below show, it was evidently to Sir Thomas that Evelyn turned for advice in gardening matters during the years he was making his garden at Sayes Court.[1] Sir Thomas was eight years older than Evelyn, and the letters are those of a kindly elderly expert to a younger enthusiast.

Bettisfield, August 22, 1668

SIR,

I have had so much company with me here this summer and so many other avocations that I had scarce time to scribble out these enclosed papers for you. They are but common observations, but true ones, and most of the famed secrets for ameliorating flowers will not prove so. If you pardon my defects and accept of my desires to serve you I have my ends. Some other receipts I intended you as for making cherry wine and cowslip wine but I have mislaid them; if I can find them in time I shall send them to you. I judged it of no purpose to speak of more sorts of flowers than I have done, these being the choicest and so much having been printed of other sorts. I long extremely to see your work public, having so spacious and delicious a field to walk in and your knowledge being so exact though general, that great pleasure as well as benefit must needs arise to the peruser thereof. Sir, the bearer hereof is one Mr Eyton of the Inner Temple a friend of mine as his father was of your eldest brother's; he is a young florist and planter and desires to be recommended to your acquaintance as I very heartily do to you, being a very civil ingenious person. My humble service to your lady, I beseech you, and to my noble friend Sir Richard Browne, and accept of the same to yourself from

Sir

Your most humble and faithful servant

THO. HANMER.

[1] John Evelyn acquired possession of Sayes Court, Deptford, from his father-in-law, Sir Richard Browne, in 1652, and under the date 17th January 1653 he notes in his Diary: "I began to set out the ovall garden at Sayes Court which was before a rude orchard and all the rest an intire field of 100 acres without any hedge except the hither holly hedge joyning to the banke of the mount walk. This was the beginning of all the succeeding gardens, walks, groves, enclosures and plantations there."

Bettisfield, August 21st, 1671

SIR,

I send you herewith some rootes of severall sorts: the bears ears and some of the anemones and ranunculus are very good but the tulips (except Agat Hanmer *and the* Ariana *and some others) are not extraordinary; indeed my garden affords not now such varieties of rare tulips as I had formerly; most of my best died the first yeare I came to live at this place, and I have not furnisht my selfe anew, because I thinke neither this ayer nor earth agrees with them.*

I suppose your flower garden, being new, is not very large, and therefore I send you not many things at this tyme, and I wish the beares eares doe not dry too much before you receave them; they will be a fortnight at least before they come to Deptford, and therefore sett them as soone as may be, and water them well (if it raine not) for three or fower days, and plant them not in too hott a sun. I thought once to have ventur'd some gilliflowers, having two years since raised some very good ones from seed (wh I never did before, nor I thinke never shall againe, because the wett in England hinders the ripening of the seed more than in Holland and Flanders) but there is such store of excellent ones all about London that I had not the confidence to adventure any to your view;—and I doubted whether being soe long on the way would not kill them.

Sir, I wish I were better able to serve you either in these bagatelles or more weighty occasions: I should with great alacrity and satisfaction, I assure you, lay hold on all opportunityes to express myselfe how really I am

Sr

Yor affectionate faithfull servant

THO. HANMER.

My wife and my selfe humbly present or services to your worthy lady, and your selfe, as also to my noble friend Sr Richard

Browne. I convey this letter and the box to you by my son Tom Hanmer, who is constantly at his chamber in ffig-tree Court in the Inner Temple, and can send your commands to mee at any tyme. You will find in the box some very good bear's ears seed, which you know better to sow and order than I can direct.

Further, Evelyn's *Kalendarium Hortense* has hitherto ranked as the earliest gardening calendar in the English language, but Sir Thomas Hanmer's volume, dated 1653, contains one written eleven years earlier, which now takes the first place.[1] It was written four years before the publication of John Evelyn's first book, *The French Gardener.* John Evelyn's great work—*The Plan of a Royal Garden*—was never completed. Only fragments —*Acetaria* and *Kalendarium Hortense*—were published, and his other gardening books, *The French Gardener* and *The Compleat Gardener*, are translations. But Sir Thomas Hanmer's *Garden Book* is an original work, and every page testifies to the knowledge and enthusiasm of the author. There is no mention in his book of knots and embroidered parterres and so forth[2]; it is evident that he took as little interest in these as the great gardeners of to-day take in colour schemes. His interest was concentrated on the plants, and herein lies his appeal to modern gardeners.

It is pleasant to visualize the garden to which Sir Thomas devoted himself. It was probably a square or rectangular enclosure, for according to the authoritative writers of the period, notably Bacon,[3] Parkinson and Worledge, a square enclosure was usual in this country. The pleasure garden was doubtless adorned with at least one fountain and probably several statues,

[1] For Sir Thomas Hanmer's garden calendar see pages 144-151 inclusive.

[2] Sir Thomas, however, mentions knots and parterres in a paper evidently intended to be the preface of his *Garden Book*. See page xviii.

[3] "The garden is best to be square encompassed on all four sides with a stately arched hedge."—Francis Bacon, *Of Gardens.*

"The foure square forme is most usually accepted with all and doth best agree to any man's dwelling."—John Parkinson, *Paradisus.*

and laid out in rectangular beds (slightly raised and supported by coloured boards, tiles or stones) planted with flowers and divided by well-kept gravelled or sanded paths; beyond, a "wilderness", *i.e.* walks between clipped hedges of holly, yew or bay, or alleys planted on either side with elms, firs, scarlet oaks, pines, cypresses, etc. These walks were a great feature in the gardens of this period and must have been most attractive. It is not known exactly when the custom was introduced of clipping trees, such as yews and holly, so as to leave the trunks bare up to a height of about twelve feet and then allowing them to grow naturally, but this method was fashionable during the latter part of the seventeenth and early years of the eighteenth century. Sometimes the branches above the bare trunks were pleached and clipped so as to form a solid wall of greenery.[1] These walks must have had a quaint charm of their own, and as the illustrations show, they were a perfect setting for the costumes of the period. There is no mention of topiary work in Sir Thomas Hanmer's book, although this was the period when it was so fashionable, and I think it more likely that this great plant-lover allowed his trees and shrubs to grow naturally.

The following passage, found by Sir Thomas's descendant, John Lord Hanmer, amongst his ancestor's MSS, was obviously intended by the former to be the preface to his *Garden Book*. Herein one of the greatest authorities of his generation sets forth his opinions on the state of gardening in England during the latter half of the seventeenth century:

> As soon as peace hath introduced plenty and wealth into a country men quickly apply themselves to pleasures, and by degrees endeavour to improve them to the height. Amongst the innocent ones, persons of quality and ingenuity have in all ages delighted themselves with beautiful gardens, whose chiefest ornaments are choice flowers, trees and plants; after which rarities the French and

[1] This method is depicted in the plate of St John's College in W. Williamson's *Oxonia Depicta* (1717).

Dutch have for some years been most diligent enquirers and collectors, as the Italians and Germans before them, and since our late war many of this nation. The rich among us now are not satisfied with good houses and parks, or handsome avenues and issues to and from their dwellings, their ambition and curiosity extends also to very costly embellishments of their gardens, orchards and walks, and some spare no charge, amongst other things, in procuring the rarest flowers and plants to set them forth withal.

Yet though this way of beautifying and divertisement comes apace into fashion, few know how to choose well their materials of this kind, or to order and dispose of them, and so are at much charge in vain, their gardeners being also for the most part very inexpert and dull. To remedy this in some measure the ensuing Catalogue of choice plants, yet such as will bear our climate, is exhibited to the public with short directions for their preservation and increase not meddling with their medicinal qualities whereof so many volumes have been written. The tract is as little as may be, the intention being only for a temporary help to the lovers of this way of delight; foreseeing that perfecter things will come forth. Thus much more is not unfit to be premised; that not only the whole designs or laying out of garden grounds are much different from what our fathers used, but the inward part or works also. In these days the borders are not hedged about with privet, rosemary or other such herbs which hide the view and prospect, and nourish hurtful worms and insects, nor are standard fruit trees suffered to grow so high or thick as to shadow and cumber the soyle, but all is now commonly near the house laid open and exposed to the sight of the rooms and chambers, and the knots and borders are upheld only with very low coloured boards or stone, or tile. If the ground be spacious, the next adjacent quarters or *parterres*, as the French call them, are often of fine turf, but as low as any green to bowl on; cut out curiously into embroidery of flowers and shapes of arabesques, animals or birds, or *feuillages*, and the small alleys or intervals filled with several coloured sands and dust with much art, with but few flowers in such knots, and those only such as grow very low, least they spoil the beauty of the embroidery.

Those remote from habitation are compartments, as they call them, which are knots also, and borders destined for flowers, yet sometimes intermixed with grasswork, and on the outside beautified with vases on pedistals, or dwarf cypresses, firs, and other greens which will endure our winters, set uniformly, at reasonable distances from each other, and in these great grounds beyond are either labyrinths with hedges cut to a man's height, or thickets for birds cut through with gravely walks, or you have variety of alleys set with elms, limes, abeles, firs and pines, with fountains, cascades and statues. These large grounds are commonly a third part longer than broad, and cannot well be less than two or three hundred yards in length; but it suffices most gentlemen to have only a square or oblong piece of ground of three score or eighty yards, with handsome gravel walks, and all florists have, besides the embroidery and compartments where their guests amuse themselves, a little private seminary, to keep such treasures as are not to be exposed to every one's view, and a winter house for shelter of plants, of which more hereafter, etc.

It is interesting to realize that of the flowers of which Sir Thomas writes many, now amongst the most familiar denizens of our gardens, had only been introduced during the previous fifty years—tulips, the crown imperial, several of the most notable narcissi (Tradescant's "great double narcissus", Willmer's narcissus, and "Robinus his Narcissus soe-called from that famous florist of the name in Paris"), martagon lilies, the yellow crocus, double hepaticas, lychnis, lobelia cardinalis, nasturtiums, marvel of Peru, etc.

To tulips Sir Thomas accords the first place amongst bulbous flowers and he writes of them at considerable length. This is not surprising, for the tulip mania was then at its height. The tulip he describes as "the Queene of Bulbous plants whose Flower is beautifull in its figure and most rich and admirable in colours and wonderfull in variety of markings". Like Parkinson he mentions many of the delightful old names, and he makes the noteworthy statement that

> wee did value in England only such as were well stript with purples and other redds and pure white; but now, within a yeare or two, we esteemed (as the French doe) any mixtures of odde

colours . . . and such as are markt with any yellows or Isabellas[1] are much prized.

Tulip beds, he observes, should be about four feet wide and raised in the centre "that all the flowers may bee seene the better". Raising beds in this fashion was a common custom in France. I like the charming passage concerning the enthusiastic tulip-lover in spring: "And now the Florists fly about to see and examine and take the chiefe pleasure of gardens. . . ."[2] John Lord Hanmer in his *Memorials* quotes notes on tulips[3] from

[1] A full list of the words used in describing the colours of flowers in the seventeenth century will be found on page xxvii.

[2] Page 24.

[3] *Notes from Sir Thomas Hanmer's Pocket-book*

"Tulips sent to Sir J. Trevor 1654. 1 Peruchot 1 Admiral Euchuysen 1 of my Angelicas 1 Comisetta 1 Omen 1 of my best Dianas, all very good bearing rootes, sent by my wife from Haulton.

"June 1655. Lord Lambert, I sent him by Rose a very great mother-root of Agate Hanmer.

"Lord Lambert hath the yellow jasmyn, the double striped pomegranate, many Narcissi of Constantinople and Algiers. Mr Bodyngton, a merchant furnishes Lord Lambert with these varieties.

"Walker of St James's has many Virginia plants. The locust tree, he saith, bears a tayle of white flowers: it comes from Virginia.

"June 1656. Tulipes given to Ld. Lambert: Belle Isabelle, Belle Susanne etc.

"Tulipes then given Mrs Thurloe: 2 Von Velzens, 1 Gen Zugman etc. Tulipes then given Mr Hygens: 1 Peach Morillion etc.

"In my last letter I wrote to Moryn [the French nurseryman of that name in Paris] (P. Moryn le Jeusne dit troisième) I would give but 16 pistoles for the anemonies and ranunculus I sent for in my first letter. He asked 18 pistoles."

John Lord Hanmer quotes further notes on the subject of tulip culture from MSS left by Sir Thomas:

"Set them in the ground about the full moon in September about four inches asunder and under four inches deep, set the early ones where the sun in the spring may come hot on them. Set the later kinds where the noon sun may not be too fierce on them. Let the earth be mold taken from the fields, or where woodstacks have been, and mix it with a fourth part or more of sand. Make your beds at least half a yard thick of this mold. Tulips live best planted alone, but you may put some anemonies with them on the outside the beds if they be raised high and round. They will come up in December and January and the early sorts flower in the latter end of March, and beginning of April, the other a fortnight or more after them. Set the mother-roots by themselves, and the young off-sets by themselves. The new varieties of tulips come from sowing their seeds, but the seedlings will be five years at least before they bear a flower. Keep old strong roots for seed, of such kinds as have blue cup and purple chives, and are striped with pure white, and carnations or gridelines, or murreys. The single cups with blue cups or bottoms, and purple chives will most of them parrach or stipe, and will stand two years unremoved when the roots are old."

Sir Thomas Hanmer's pocket-book, and there is one entry referring to "a very great mother-root of Agate Hanmer" sent to Lord Lambert in June 1655. Lord Lambert was the Parliamentarian general already mentioned.[1] Sir Thomas says he sent this root "by Rose". This was presumably John Rose,[2] who in Charles II's reign was appointed head of the royal gardens. "Agate Hanmer", John Lord Hanmer states, was a tulip first grown in this country at Bettisfield; its colours were gris de lin, crimson and white. Rea in his *Flora Ceres and Pomona* says:

> Agot Hanmer is a beautiful Flower, of three good colours, pale gredeline, deep scarlet and pure white, commonly well parted, striped, agoted and excellently placed, abiding constant to the last, with the bottom and Tamis blew. This gallant Tulip hath its name from that ingenious lover of these rarities, *Sir Thomas Hanmer*, who first brought it into *England*, from whose free community, my self and others partake the delight of this noble Flower.

John Lord Hanmer quotes also notes in Sir Thomas's handwriting on the tulips he grew himself. The latter half of these notes are particularly interesting, for they are the only record that has come down to us showing how the flower-beds in a late seventeenth-century garden were actually planted.

> 1660. *Flowers in the Great Garden. December. Bettisfield*
>
> In the first of the four little bordered beds in the midst of the bordered knot:—The first is that on the right hand path next to the house; the ranks begin at the end next the house, from the north to the south.
>
> Tulips.
>
> First rank—1. Good marked Mother; 2. Dentelle Teoras Mother; 3. New Hazard Mother; 4. Widow Mother.
>
> Second rank—1. Proteus Mother; 2. Tetlier Mother; 3. Pelack Prince Mother; 4. Puissant Mother.
>
> Third Rank—1. Bonne; 2. Carthago; 3. Piece a portee; 4. A marked tulip.

[1] See page ix.

[2] John Rose, who had been in the service of the Earl of Essex, was sent to Versailles to study under Le Nôtre. He was appointed head of the royal gardens in succession to Andrew Mollet.

Fourth Rank—1. Charmante; 2. Olympia; 3. Agate Poictevin; 4. New Hazard.

Fifth Rank—1. Saturn; 2. Carthago; 3. Hair colour; 4. L'abilly.

Sixth Rank—1. Polonois; 2. Memorable; 3. Erimanthe; 4. Trois couleurs.

Seventh Rank—1. Jaspee Anglaise; 2. A good marked one.

In the two further corners of the first bed are two colchicum chives, and in the next two corners two roots of Liere de Paris anemone. The second little bed is the further of the two on the right hand. In the middle of this bed is one Double Crown Imperial. In the end are six rows of Iris raised from seed by Rea; also polyanthuses and daffodils. In the four corners of this bed are four roots of good anemones.

The third little bed is the first of the four on the left hand.

First Rank—1 hyacinth of Lisle, a good watchet colour; 6 jonquils; 1 hyacinth of Peru.

Second Rank—6 double yellow jonquils, and 1 black fritellary in the middle.

Third Rank—1 gray fritellary; 6 red Deuscanius; 1 gray fritellary.

Fourth Rank—2 narcissus, pale wings and yellow cups; 2 musarte oriental narcissi.

Fifth Rank—2 great white Argires; 2 Belles de Brussells.

Sixth Rank—2 Belles de Val narcissi, all yellow; 2 yellow Argires narcissi.

Seventh Rank—2 Belles Fournière narcissi, all yellow, greater flower than the Argires; 2 Constantinople narcissi, double, bore not.

Eighth Rank—2 Belle Selmane narcissi, right dear ones; 1 Bel del Vine narcissus, small white and yellow cup.

Ninth Rank—1 colchicum vernale; 3 Iris dell' Abbaye, one died; 2 colchicum vernale.

Tenth Rank—1 gray fritillare; 6 white Deuscanius; 1 gray fritillare.

Eleventh Rank—6 double yellow jonquils.

Twelfth Rank—1 hyacinth of Peru; 6 jonquils; 1 hyacinth of Lisle.

The fourth bed, being the further of the four little beds from the house of the left hand.

First Rank—The Kind Mother, and an offset by it; 2. Dentelle Floras Mother; 3. Perseus Mother; 4. good marked.

Second Rank—Dorothy of Holland; 2. Agate Bizarre Mother and offset; 3. Barbancon's Mother; 4. Agate Bizarre.
Third Rank—Supreme Mother; 2. Oronte Mother; 3. Feuille-straite, great offset; 4. Deepe offset.
Fourth Rank—Agate Poictevin; 2. Babancon's or Carthago Mother; 3. Memorabile Mother and offset; 4. Charlottes.
Fifth Rank—Seisan Agate Mother; 2. Cupsidon Mother; 3. Puissant Mother; 4. Two Isabel or Agate Poictevins.
Sixth Rank—New Hazard Mother; 2. Amazone; 3. Oriental Moryn; 4. Pamises.
Seventh Rank—1. Passze Belyn; 2. General Norris; 3. Clytus; 4. Good marked offset.
Eighth Rank—1 Mahomet; 2 L'Abcile; 3. Carthago Mother; 4. Belle Isabel.
Ninth Rank—1. Dieppe; 2. Phoenix; 3. Feuillstraite; 4. Aurora.
Tenth Rank—1. Trois Couleurs; 2. Agate Hanmer; 3. Best Anglaises; 4. Bonnes Bigeures.
Eleventh Rank—Proteus Mother; 2. Heliodore; 3. Radigonele; 4. Altiguife or Saturn.
Twelfth Rank—1. Guymet; 2. Velours; 3. La Feu; 4. Trigen.
Thirteenth Rank—1. Royal Vesta; 2. Viceroy; 3. Isabella; 4. Zuyman.

All the little bordered beds, besides the four little middle ones of that quarter are full of anemones on the outsides and tulips and narcissuses in the midst, with some gilly flowers and some buses at the ends of the beds and cyclamens at the four corners.
The border under the south wall in the Great Garden is full of good anemones, and near the musk rose are two roots of the daffodil of Constantinople from Rea and a martagon pomponium.
In the border under my Lady's closet are anemones and two pieces of Lière de Paris and 2 double yellow ranunculuses and a great root of Georgina tulips and a root of Queen May and some tulips I know not what and 2 good red cowslips and 2 roots of two sorts of rare Virginian martagons.
In the border under the stack of chimneys by the door are tulips and crocuses.
In the border under the west wall by the court door are offsets of all manner of tulips and anemones.
In the border under the north wall are beares ears (auriculas) and

> cowslips; some of the beares ears are marked which came from Rose and Tom Turner, those that came from Rose last are set by the corner next to the court wall, by the duke cherry. One faire Frances, two purple Frances, one red bud, four roses olive, five Yeomen of Kent, six Virgin's gift.
>
> In the border under the wall within the garden by the grasse walk are several roots of fraxinellas, and Virginia spider worts and primroses and some anemonies and daffodils.

Sir Thomas treats next of narcissi, the most interesting he mentions being Tradescant's double narcissus, Willmer's and "Robinus his Narcissus". The two first named have been grown in English gardens for three centuries. Tradescant's rose-shaped narcissus is still one of our largest doubles and commemorates John Tradescant the elder, gardener to Charles I, and "the rose and lily queen" Henrietta Maria. Parkinson in his *Paradisus* gives a full account of the origin of the name Willmer's double daffodil[1] which should have been called after Vincent Sion, "an industrious and worthy lover of faire flowers". "Robinus his Narcissus" was named, as Sir Thomas Hanmer says, after "that famous florist in Paris". This was of course Jean Robin, Keeper of the King's garden in Paris, to whom there are frequent references in Gerard's *Herball* and Parkinson's *Paradisus*.

Before treating of hyacinths Sir Thomas writes of various bulbs newly imported, particularly amaryllis. John Lord Hanmer says:

> In 1655, some one appears, by a note which I have lately found,

[1] "We first had it from Vincent Sion, borne in Flanders, dwelling on the Bank side, in his lives time, but now dead, an industrious and worthy lover of faire flowers, who cherished it in his garden for many yeares, without bearing of any flowers untill the yeare 1620, that having flowred with him (and hee not knowing of whom he received it, not having ever seene the like flower before) he sheweth it to Mr John de Franqueville, of whom he supposed he had received it (for from beyond Sea he never received any) who findeth it to bee a kinde never seene or knowne to us before, caused him to respect it the more, as it is well worthy. And Mr George Wilmer of Stratford Bowe Esquire in his lives time having likewise received it of him (as myselfe did also) would needes appropriate it to himselfe, as if he were the first founder thereof, and call it by his owne name Wilmer's double Daffodill, which since hath so continued."—John Parkinson, *Paradisus*.

to have sent Sir Thomas an Amaryllis lily from Barbados; it was received and planted at Bettisfield in that year, and was esteemed a great curiosity, but it would not flower more than once; the stems are described as about two feet high, the flowers of a pinkish orange hue, and the leaves, only larger, like those of daffodils; the plant is common enough in many varieties. I believe that from Barbadoes is called Equestris.

Cornutus, to whom Sir Thomas refers, is the celebrated French botanist Jacques Cornutus, author of *Canadensium Plantarum Alearumque Nondum Editorum Historia* (1635).[1]

After hyacinths comes a section on "great bulbous irises" and then on "small bulbous irises". This section on irises is particularly valuable, for Sir Thomas incorporates a catalogue of sixty-nine varieties drawn up by Monsieur Moryn, "a famous Florist in France". This must be the earliest iris catalogue extant, and it is interesting to note that in the seventeenth century standards in flowers were sometimes called "sails".[2] Sir Thomas describes only three kinds of crown imperial—the single orange "of an ill dead orange colour", the double orange "yet rare", and the single yellow "more rare". Unlike Parkinson, he was evidently not an enthusiastic admirer of this plant. The date of its introduction into England is unknown, for though Shakespeare mentions it, Gerard describes it as a rare and strange plant.

Amongst the other pleasant old-fashioned flowers seldom seen in modern gardens (to our loss), Sir Thomas grew *lychnis chalcedonica, lobelia cardinalis,* dittany and "dragons" (*arum dracunculus*). *Lychnis chalcedonica* is generally said to have been introduced in Elizabeth's reign, but it was probably introduced long before, possibly during the Crusades, for in nearly every European language its old name is Cross of Jerusalem. Cross of Jerusalem is the old English name, and in French, Spanish and Italian it is similarly named. The old Portuguese name is Cruz

[1] See page 32.
[2] See page 38.

de Malta, probably because the shape of the flower is suggestive of a Maltese cross. *Lobelia cardinalis*, one of the finest and most brilliantly coloured of all autumn-flowering plants, is another treasure still more seldom seen. Parkinson calls it a "brave plant", and James Justice, writing over a century later, says "it excells all other flowers I ever knew in the richness of its colour". The name "lobelia" was bestowed on this North American plant in Louis XIV's reign by Charles Plumier, the French botanist, in honour of Matthias Lobel. Dittany has always had a reputation of being a mystic plant, and formerly it was used by witches in their concoctions. Apart from its interesting associations it is a pity it is so seldom grown, for the flowers are curiously attractive. "Dragons" Sir Thomas probably grew not only on account of their handsome appearance, but for use, for in the sixteenth and seventeenth centuries "dragons" were grown in every garden, both for medicinal use and for the starch they furnished. Gerard says "the most pure and white starch is made from it", and he adds: "it is most hurtfull to the hands of the laundress that hath the handling of it; for it chappeth, blistereth and maketh the handes rough and rugged and withall smarting". There has always been a tradition that it was a Dutch woman who first taught the English laundresses the use of this plant, for starching the immense ruffs then worn. The roots were also used in making soap.

It is interesting to note the words Sir Thomas uses to describe the colours of flowers, for our seventeenth-century ancestors were far more accurate in this respect than we are. For instance, "pale pink" is frequently used nowadays to describe a flower which is not pale pink at all, but what in olden days would have been described as "pale murrey", *i.e.* a very pale mulberry colour. The best instance I know is Parkinson's description of the beautiful Maiden's Blush rose—"of a bright pale murrey colour". This exactly describes the lovely faint colour with which this rose is suffused. Nor have we any word corresponding to "watchet"—the blue of a summer sky. This rare colour in flowers is described nowadays as "pale blue", but the blue of a summer sky is something far more vivid than mere "pale blue" and we have no modern word whereby to describe it. The following list comprises the words in common use in the seventeenth century to describe the colours of flowers:

Amaranthe—purple.
Aurora—deep orange.
Bertino—blue-grey.
Celadon—pale green.
Furille-mort—possibly feuille-morte (dead leaf colour).
Gilvus—very pale red.
Grideline—flax-grey. From the French *gris de lin*, 'grey of flax'. Littré explains it as 'a colour partaking of white and red'. Sir William Temple in his *Garden of Epicurus* describes the Burgundy grape as 'a grizelin or pale red'.
Isabella—greyish yellow. In Murray's *Dictionary* the explanation that the colour derived its name from the Archduchess Isabella (who vowed she would not change her stockings till the siege of Ostend was raised, 1601-1604) is shown to be absurd. For the word is used in the Inventory of Queen Elizabeth's wardrobe (1600)—'one rounde gowne of Isabella colour satten . . . set with silver spangles'.
Minimme—dun colour. According to Littré, from the colour of the Minim Friar's robe.
Murrey—mulberry.
Quoist—probably a variant of queest—the colour of a dove's breast. 'The stockdove is also termed by us a Quees or Quiese.' (R. Holme, *Armoury*, 1688.)
Watchet—sky blue.

There are frequent references to French florists and French methods in Sir Thomas's book. These are noteworthy, for apart from the fact that so keen a gardener naturally made excellent use of his long sojourns abroad, we owed much in this country both to French and Dutch growers. Italian influence in the sixteenth and seventeenth centuries is difficult to estimate. In Elizabeth's reign every young man of any standing visited Italy, and the magnificent fountains which were such a marked feature in our gardens during the following century were doubtless due to Italian influence. But it is a remarkable and interesting fact that whereas some two hundred Italian books were translated into English and published between 1547 and 1600, no Italian gardening book was translated. From the French and Dutch, however, we had much to learn, and some of our most important gardening manuals of Tudor and Stuart days were translations from French and Dutch originals, notably Leonard Mascall's *Book of the Art and manner howe to plant and graffe*, Richard Surflet's *Countrie Farme*, Crispin de Passe's *Garden of Flowers* and John Evelyn's *Compleat Gard'ner*. Further, we owe a great debt to the Huguenot refugees from France and the Low Countries; there were numerous skilled gardeners amongst them and they established celebrated market gardens at Battersea and Bermondsey. They are said also to have established the first flower societies in England, the most noted being that at Norwich and the earliest at Spitalfields.

Sir Thomas's lists of fruit trees are lengthy and give us an excellent idea of the well-stocked fruit garden of the mid-seventeenth century. Great attention was given to fruit-growing in Commonwealth days, and the earliest book of importance on this subject was published during this period, namely Ralph Austen's *Treatise of Fruit Trees* (1653). Of exotic fruits, oranges were a fashionable cult and Sir Thomas writes at some length about them. I like his description of the scent of the flowers—"deliciously and comfortably sweet".

Not the least interesting section of his book is that devoted to viticulture. Vineyards had declined greatly in early Stuart times, and Parkinson in his *Paradisus* ascribes the cause to the change in our climate (how modern this seems!) and the dissolution of the monasteries, the monks being the skilful growers. In Charles II's reign, however, viticulture attracted considerable attention, the two most noted books of the period being those by William Hughes, *The Complete Vineyard* (1665), and John Rose's *English Vineyard Vindicated* (1666), with a preface by Philocepos (John Evelyn).[1] John Rose, who is credited with having presented Charles I with the first pineapple ripened in England, had studied in France under Le Nôtre, and subsequently was appointed head of the royal gardens in this country in succession to Andrew Mollet. Sir Thomas Hanmer's section on viticulture is every whit as practical and interesting as the two small treatises cited above. John Rose sent Sir Thomas two vines; one being the Lombardy vine, "as Rose calls it, the King's gardener, beares a faire red grape wh. the King loves". John Lord Hanmer says Rose sent his ancestor also "the right Rhenish grape", both these vines being personally recommended to Sir Thomas by King Charles II.

Sir Thomas was evidently as profoundly interested in his vines and fruit trees as in his pleasure garden. I quote the following from John Lord Hanmer's *Memorials*:

Fruit Trees in the Great Garden at Bettisfield 1660 *from a Memorandum in the Handwriting of Sir Thomas Hanmer*

Against the South wall are one Apricocke from Mr Rea, three Apricockes from London, one peache from a French stone, raised at Bettisfield 1660 and two red-heart cherries from Trevallyn. In the corner next to the turf walk one pear from Bowen, I think a bergamot.

Against the West wall there, from the south wall to the door, all plums from Colonel Jeffrys, except one double-flowered cherry, and one morocco plum next the door; on the other side the door, first a bullen plum, then a Turkey plum, then a Ring plum, then a Catalonia plum, and a Duke cherry, a cornelian.

Against the North Wall these plums from Trevallyn, viz the

[1] John Rose's treatise was published subsequently with John Evelyn's *French Gardener* (1669, 1675 and 1691).

Apricocke plum and the orange, and one plum from Colonel Jeffrys. Against the East wall in the Great Garden, may cherries, a carnation cherry, about the middle of the wall, a duke cherry at the end, close by the North Wall, a cornelian cherry from Rea marbled, and a Turkey plum from Rea.

Against the stack of chimneys and the wall bet^{n} the chimney and the door are a rare vine, a vine from K. Eyton, a Bon Chrétien pear and a peach from a French stone raised at Bettisfield 1660.

Against the wall by the green turf walk are peaches that were removed from Haulton which came thither from London and one peach raised at Bettisfield from a French stone 1660, which peach is next to the Great Garden door next the orchard; there are also 2 heart cherries and a cornelian tree at the end by the yew tree.

Against the wall by the gravelly walk towards the highway are all peaches, two of which viz the first next to the Court Gate is a Roman peach and the third from the gate is a nutmeg peach; the next are all peaches from stones set by me at Lewisham and removed thence to Bettisfield.

In the little court with the stone stairs against the little garden wall are three peaches from Mr Bate viz a Morillo peach next the little Garden Door, then a Newington peach and then a Persian peach. Against the other wall, over against these peaches are two plums from Rea.

In the little garden against the south wall, beginning from the house, are four common apricockes then an early apricocke then a bellowes peach near the corner.

Against the east wall of the little garden by the two sycamores are, beginning from the south wall, first three peaches raised 1660 at Bettisfield from French stones, then a peach de Pau, then a Savoy peach.

These careful notes show the intense interest Sir Thomas took in every detail pertaining to his garden. Like his book they throw a light not merely on the character of one of the notabilities of Stuart and Commonwealth days, but on a side of the everyday life of the period which it is pleasant to visualise. For Sir Thomas was a typical English country gentleman. He loved his home and garden and took delight in the simple pleasures of the country.

ELEANOUR SINCLAIR ROHDE

Sir Thomas Hanmer

VAN DYCK

A NOTE ON THE TEXT

"But the iniquity of oblivion blindly scattereth her poppy, and deals with the Memory of men without distinction to merit of Perpetuity." These words of another Sir Thomas, so nearly of an age with our author, are truly apt on this occasion. Sir Thomas Hanmer has lain buried under a drift of poppy petals for nearly three centuries, while Sir Thomas Browne has been beloved of poets and scholars in each generation. And now pure chance has dispelled the long obscurity and the unknown stands before us, in his gay cavalier clothes, with his "littel Memoriall booke, writing downe the name of every flower", as fresh and unfaded as they.

The MS came into the hands of Messrs Davis & Orioli in the ordinary way of business early in 1932, and might well have been sold as casually as it was bought. It is a thick quarto, bound in plain brown calf, in no way spectacular or likely to attract attention. Curiosity, however, got the better of me, and I gave myself up to deciphering page after page of the faded brown script, somewhat furtively, such occupations being usually considered a dereliction from duty. It was soon clear that the MS was more important than had been supposed, as being obviously a complete book, and not a series of random jottings, and I began to wonder whether the work had ever been published. To my surprise I found it had not (though by a reference to "the Reader" it is clear that the author intended it to be), and the enthusiasm of experts confirmed our impulse to give Sir Thomas Hanmer's book to the world as he would have wished.

The two pages of the MS here reproduced give a very slight idea of the difficulties this involved. I told the publishers that it would have been more representative to show the worst pages rather than the best, but the result would certainly not have been so charming. Though the author's handwriting is always beautiful and regular, most pages are scrawled through and through with corrections and insertions, and a few have been burnt into holes, though luckily this never obliterates more than half a word. On page 158 there is a square bracket which marks the only word, out of 40,000, which remained completely illegible, in spite of every effort. In this case even Mr Murray's great dictionary, to which I often resorted gratefully, could not save me. The other square brackets enclose marginal notes which were clearly added at a later date. Hanmer himself left only one sentence unfinished, that on Medlars, page 156. We shall never know whether this was an oversight, or mere inability to be inspired by that uninspiring fruit.

In transcribing the original manuscript I have tried to preserve the orthography and punctuation as faithfully as possible. This has led to a number of inconsistencies, as Hanmer rarely spelt the same word twice alike, though it were in the very same sentence. As to his use of capitals, it seems that they often express emphasis, at other times they appear to be entirely capricious. But the general effect of all such differences is to enhance the writer's individuality very strongly, as on page 12 where, in his description of the making of a *hott bed*, he appears to be almost breathless with excitement.

A word about the portraits. I found that Sir Thomas, and his lady too, had been painted by the ubiquitous Van Dyck (Sir Thomas's position of cup-bearer to Charles I would sufficiently explain the choice of painter), but the portrait itself had been destroyed in a fire at Barton Hall in Suffolk in 1914. Messrs Quaritch have very kindly lent the block from this Van Dyck portrait, which was made for a book they published in 1908: *Portraits in Suffolk Houses*, by the Rev Edmund Farrer. A descendant of the author's, Sir C. H. W. Bunbury, Bart (Sir Thomas's granddaughter, Susan, became Lady Bunbury), has lent the miniature portrait by Cooper which has been reproduced in colour as frontispiece. It shows Sir Thomas as an older man, yet with the same carriage of the head, a similar forthright, fearless, somewhat challenging expression. I fancy the younger portrait shows us more of the courtier, the young blade, while in the elder one we see the cultured country gentleman (a friend of Cowley and Sir William Davenant), the meticulous gardener, noting each flower, where and how it blew, and taking infinite pains to secure them from "the inclemencie of our English wynters".

The first part of the MS book, as one complete work, ends on page 151 with the Remembrances, and occupies 248 pages. After that follow a number of miscellaneous notes, from which we have selected those which seem most proper to include here. This part of the manuscript is extremely hard to read. There are notes copied from printed books, or passed from mouth to mouth, as "had by Mr Kenricke Eyton from the Earle of Salisburyes gardener", or "Of Melons, out of Sir H. Plat's booke of Flowers" (*Floraes Paradise*, London, 1608); there are notes on pigeons, with the prices he gave for them (ranging apparently from 1s to "an Angell and upwards for a paire"); and lastly there are the exact descriptions of where each flower was set in certain years, "against the corner of the stacke of the parlor chimney", "at the south end of the bed, by the doore, towards the stable", etc. And on the first two pages of the book are little notes in diary form, occupying about a square inch of space each, of which surely the most grateful to the author must have been: "My grandchild Thomas Hanmer was born at Bettisfield on Monday betwixt ten and eleven at night being the twenty-fourth of September 1677". This was the Speaker of the House of Commons, who lived to make his grandfather's name a well-known one.

I can only hope that this belated publication will prove the gardener's name as illustrious as that of the statesman.

IVY ELSTOB

Of the DISTINCTIONS of FLOWERS. 1

FLOWERS are vsually distinguisht either by their ORDINARY naturall SEASONS of BLOWING in our Climate, or by the DIFFERENT sorts of their ROOTES. The Seasons they most constantly obserue are the fower Quarters of the yeare, yet some beare their flowers not only in one, but in two or more of them. Many blow in the SPRING which after the Latine are called by writers, VERNALL, more in the SOMMER moneths, called ÆSTIVALL, some in AUTUMNE and therefore named AUTUMNALL, and a few only in WINTER, and soe as the former after the Latine words, tearmed HYEMALL.

Generally Authors who distinguish FLOWERS by their ROOTES, make but THREE SORTS of them, BULBOUS. TUBEROUS, and FIBROUS, but I shall adde one difference more, which I thinke as considerable as any of the other and that is GLANDULOUS, and thus shall they bee here treated of and not according to their Seasons of Flowring, though they shall also bee particulerly mentioned.

OF BULBOUS FLOWERS.

The Flowers in highest esteeme now amongst vs are such as haue those ROOTES wee call BULBOUS, of which there are different kinds both for the figure, and greatnes, but all of

OF CHOOSING SEED, and of SOWING and ORDERING it.

The best Seed is the most weighty, and is had from the lustiest and most vigorous stimms. Wee vse to crop of flowers of such kinds as are many on a stalke to make the other seede the better, and haue the more vertue and such wee find vsually in the Lower seed vessells of the stalks. Bee not curious to keepe the finest markt Tulipe or other rare flower for seed, vnles the kind bee strong, for better flowers are raisd from a lusty flower of one colour, then from a curious stript one of severall colours that is but weake, and commonly such will hardly afford seed at all.

Gather your Seed in faire weather, and not before it bee full ripe, which you shall perceaue by the colour of it, and by the withering of the stalke and seed case, but such seed as rises vp with downe, as Anemones, and other sorts doe, must bee watcht, and taken as soone as the downe rises, which when it is ripe one hour of hot sunshine will make it doe if it bee not gatherd presently, the least breath of aire will carry it away.

The Seed of Hardy Annualls is best sowne soone after it is ripe, of Tender Annualls in the Spring, and of all other Flowers

THE GARDEN BOOK OF
SIR THOMAS HANMER

OF THE DISTINCTIONS OF FLOWERS

FLOWERS are usually distinguisht either by their ORDINARY naturall SEASONS of BLOWING in our Climate, or by the DIFFERENT sorts of their ROOTES. The Seasons they most constantly observe are the fower Quarters of the yeare, yet some beare their flowers not only in one, but in two or more of them. Many blow in the SPRING, which after the Latine are called by writers VERNALL, more in the SOMMER moneths called AESTIVALL, some in AUTUMBE and therefore named AUTUMNALL, and a few only in WINTER, and soe as the former after the Latine words tearm'd HYEMALL. Generally Authors who distinguish FLOWERS by their ROOTES make but THREE SORTS of them, BULBOUS, TUBEROUS, and FIBROUS, but I shall adde one difference more, which I thinke as considerable as any of the other, and that is GLANDULOUS, and thus shall they bee here treated of, and not according to their Seasons of Flowering, though they shall also bee particularly mentioned.

OF BULBOUS FLOWERS

The Flowers in highest esteeme now amongst us are such as have those ROOTES *wee call* BULBOUS, *of which there are different kinds both for the figure and greatnes, but all of them resemble an Onyon more or lesse, and are made up of white fleshy tunicles which enfold one another, only the bottome or seate of the roote is of a harder substance then the rest, in which the spirit or fountain of life chiefly resides, and is thence communicated to the other parts of the bulbe, as also at the tyme of yeare to the stalkes, leaves, and flow'rs and seed.*

Our Chiefe BULBOUS *Flowers are these:*

The Tulipe, Narcissus, Iris, Crocus, Colchicum, Lilly, Crowne Imperiall, Martagon, Gladiolus, Orchis, Ornithogalum, Dens caninus, Bulbous Violet, Moly and Fritillary, and all these have smooth bulbous rootes (much like to Onyons, though not altogether soe round, for some are more pyramide like, that is sharpt upwards) except two sorts, the Lilly and the Martagon which have their bulbs scaly and not smooth in shape, much resembling an Artichoke head.

OF TUBEROUS FLOWERS

Tuberous rootes are not made up of fleshy covers as an Onyon, and other bulbes are, which may be peel'd off like to severall skins, but consist of one compact substance which is neither soe hard as the softest wood nor very tender, but firme enough. The outside is commonly of a darke or light browne color, but sometimes yellowish, and the shape of some of them is like a Turnep, roundish and flattish, but of others ragged and uneven like potatoes, earth nutts and races of ginger.

Wee have not many sorts of flowers with these rootes, the most curious are these:

Anemones, Irises, Cyclamens, Hyacynths (for there are tuberous as well as bulbous Irises and Hyacynths), Satyriums, the Hollow roote, and Dragons.

OF GLANDULOUS FLOWERS

The Glandulous rootes consist of severall glandules or lumpes, being joyn'd together at the top, and hanging in bunches, some of which are as bigg as the end of ones finger, as Peonyes, Asphodills, and Phalangium Allobrogicum, but others are much lesse, no bigger than grains of wheate, such as the Asian Ranunculus and Geranium, and of these there are no more sorts considerable than the abovementioned.

OF FIBROUS FLOWERS

All the kindes of rootes before specified when they have been a while in the earth, shoote out little threads or strings by which they are fastned and draw nourishment, and those threads are called Fibres. These strings the Bulbous, Tuberous and Glandulous rootes doe loose after their seed is perfected, and their stalkes and leaves are withered downe, for they rott away, and at the tyme of yeare of their growing againe new are againe put forth from the rootes, but these plantes which wee properly call Fibrous have these strings continually adhering to them, for though they lose some of their smaller fibers yearly, yet the greater remaine, and yearly encrease and spread abroad. These strings in some sorts hang in bunches together, and wholly make up the rootes, in some they are fastened to a woody substance, but in generall wee call all such rootes fibrous as are not either bulbous, tuberous or glandulous, though some tearme the greater fibrous sorts ligamentous, but wee shall not use that distinction.

Fibrous Rootes are of two sorts; PERENIALL & ANNUALL, *from which the whole Plants are soe denominated.*
PERENIALL *is made of the Latine word Perennis, which signifies lasting or long-lived, and pereniall flow'rs are such as usually live with us in the wynter as well as the sommer, and continue many yeares.*
ANNUALL *comes also from the Latine word Annuus, that is yearly, and such plants dye yearly every wynter, after they have perfected their seed by which they are only perpetuated, the perenialls being as well encreast and continued by the division or multiplications of their rootes as by their seed.*

Of Fibrous Perenialls we have The Gilliflower, Stocke Gilliflower, Wallflower, Beares eare, Hepatica, Lychnis, Trachelium of America, Lilly convally, Spiderwort, Valerian, Indian cane, Tufts, Maracoc or the Passion flower, Everlasting Lupine, Melanthium, Moth Mullein, Cortusa, Bellflower, Soapewort, Hesperis, Fibrous ranunculus, Hollyhocke, Cytisus, Double Pellitory, Cowslips & Primeroses, Double Featherfew, Orobus Venetus or Venetian Vetch, Hedysarum canadense, or the Suckling of Canada, Everlasting Pease, Limonium Rawolfii, Hellebore, Italian or blew Marigold, Gnaphalium Americanum, Lagopus or Hares foote, Snapdragon, Nightshade, Daisyes,

Double Ladye Smockes, Sweet William, Marsh Marigold, Columbines.

Of Annualls the best are Adonis, Africans, Marsh Mallows, Amaranthe, Scarlet Beane, Bastard Safran in Latine Carthamus, Convolvulus or Bindweede, Corneflower, French Honey-suckle, Goatesbeard, Hawkesweed, Larkespur, Cresses, Flax, Mullein, Molucca odorata, Pulsatilla, Scabious, Sonchus lanatus, Venus looking glasse, some sorts of Foxgloves, Coventry bells, Sweet Sultans, the Wonder of Peru.

These abovementioned Flowers (being as it is said of fower severall distinct kinds of Rootes) are all the sortes wee have yet knowledge of in England, worthy to bee receaved into our gardens, or at least most of them, and they are more than were enjoy'd by our ancestors, for many new kindes have within these last twenty yeares beene brought hither out of foraine parts, espetially our plantations and other countreys of the West Indyes, which were never seene here before, some whereof have required a new manner of cultivating and ordering, quite different from that of ye old English flowers, as shall bee more largely hereafter set forth and discoursed of.

Having thus mentioned the Flowers wee enjoy, we shall now speake of the Earthes fitt for them, and then generally direct how to preserve and encrease them, before wee come to treate of every kinde particularly by itself.

OF EARTHS FOR FLOWERS

Wee use two sorts of Earths in our Gardens, that is NATURALL *and* ARTIFITIALL.

The NATURALL *are only the good rich* BLACK MOLD *which is the most generally good for all kinds, but best for the Fibrous, the*

SANDY *fittest for Bulbes, and* LOAME, *a kind of fatt sand, much us'd about London, good for most rootes,* CLAY & GRAVEL *as well as* MARLE *wee almost totally reject, as too hard or wett for these tender vegetables.*
Ye ARTIFITIALL *Earthes are either* SIMPLE *or* COMPOUNDED, *and are much better than the Naturall both for Seedes and Rootes.*

The UNCOMPOUNDED *are*

1. WILLOW EARTH which is found in the trunks or bodyes of old Willowes, and is the very substance of the tree rotted with moisture into an earth, but soe light and fine as none exceeds it for the bringing up of tender seeds or rootes.
2. DUNG of Man or Beast, espetially of Cowes, but soe well rotted that it will pass through a reasonable fine sieve, and this is absolutely necessary either alone, as for Beares eares and other fibrous flowers, or mixt, as shall bee hereafter directed, for almost all flow'rs.
3. Rotted LEAVES and SPRIGS of TREES and SWEEPINGS of Houses and Streetes, all which are good for most sorts of flowers.

The COMPOUNDED *Earths* are made up of some parts of the Naturall and some parts of the Simple Artifitiall, well mixt together, which being skilfully done according to the natures of the severall plants will cause admirable effects. Tulipes prosper wonderfully in a compounded Earth of a little Sand, some dry Black Mold, and the rest Willow Earth; Cyclamens & Anemones in sifted Dung and Black Mold; Gilliflowers in rotted Leaves or Dung with some Sand; and most other fibrous rootes in the rich Artifitiall Earth that you can procure, having ever a good store of putrified dung.

The Earths being made and suited to the rootes, which must be planted as hereafter is appointed, WATERING *is necessary for many of them.*

OF WATERING FLOWERS

All Fibrous Flowers ought to bee water'd a little for three or fower days, morning & evening, after their setting or removing, if it raine not; and all such as stand in potts must bee often water'd in the Spring and beginning of sommer till they seed, and then no more; soe likewise those that stand abroad in the full earth must bee water'd in the spring sometimes when the weather is dry.

The Tuberous and Glandulous kinds neede watering only in great droughts, unless they are potted, and the Bulbous not at all, except very yong rootes.

In the Wynter and beginning of the Spring water only in the mornings, and in Sommer and Autumne in the evenings. Such plants as are hous'd need only watering in wynter, and that must bee done ever carefully, without wetting of the leaves or branches, and but seldome, and never in frosty weather.

Strong rootes may bee well water'd with a dish, but yong seedlings only with a spout-pott with small holes, from whence the water may streame forth like a gentle shower upon the earth, and not fall too violently to wash it away from the rootes, and for watering of fine seeds a pott pierc'd very small or a brush is necessary, that they bee not beaten too far into the tender mold, and there suffocated.

Gilliflowers are oft-times rotted with much watering, & many other rootes more hurt than benefited by it, therefore caution is to bee had that it bee not done overmuch at a tyme, nor too frequently.

When potted flowers are very dry, the potts are by some sett to stand in water to their middle, till they are sufficiently moistened through the holes in their bottomes, which all potts have, except such as are purposely made without any.

For Aquaticke plants, which will live constantly in water, and not long without it, Pond or River water expos'd to the sun &

ayre is the best, that drawne out of Wells is too cold untill it hath stood some tyme above ground in the ayre, the water also that issues from dunghills and such places is apt to breede wormes, and therefore to bee avoyded.

As moisture and cooleness is at some seasons necessary, soe at others in our Northerne Clymate is Covering of Rootes and seeds abroad, and housing of some sorts within doors all wynter & beginning of spring.

OF HOUSEING and COVERING of PLANTS

Many plants which come to us from hot Clymates will not endure our cold open aire abroad in Wynter, and must bee kept in tubbs or earthern vessels filled with earth to bee transportable into places of shelter as soon as the frosts begin to bee dangerous, which with us is commonly betwixt Michaelmas and Allhallowtide, where they are to remaine till the middle or end of Aprill as the yeare proves.

All that are curious in plants have a roome purposely for this use adjoyning to their garden, where not only tender flowers are put in wynter, but also delicate trees & shrubbs, such as the Orenge, Lemmon, Pomegranate, Mirtle, Jasmyne and the like, and many sorts of Greenes of which wee shall speake particularly hereafter.

This house or roome (which the French call La Serre) must bee made with judgment, otherwise it will kill more plants than it will preserve, for it is not sufficient only to withdraw these choice flowers and trees out of the sharpe open garden into a close roome, for they will perish there for want of ayre (without which nothing can live), as certainly as with cold abroad, but the roome must bee soe high and large as they may not in six moneths tyme bee choked with being constantly there, well provided with large wyndowes and doores only southwards, to bee open'd in mild weather to let in the gentle necessary ayre only, but against frosts to bee closely shut, and in very hard weather covered with matts or clothes, and sometimes in the nights warm'd with a pan of coales, a stove, or other devyce to keep a moderate heate all such violent cold nights. And thus, as I have said, all these plants that are not hardy must bee kept till the middle of Spring, and then to be sett forth a weeke or fortnight at leaste in the daytyme before they bee ventured abroad all nights.

But there are other outlandish plants that will doe very well abroad all wynter in potts set into the earth up to the brimms, under a south wall, but they must be cover'd in the hard weather with mosse or straw pretty thicke, and with glasses (shap't like bells usually) in the lesse cold seasons and nights.

OF ENCREASING or MULTIPLYING PLANTS

Plants are multiplied from their ROOTES or SEED naturally or artifitially. The encreases of Bulbous rootes are usually called by Florists Ofsetts, in French CAYEUX, and in Italian CIPOLLETTAES. The encreases of Anemones and other Fibrous rootes wee have no proper name for in English, but some call them Ofsetts, in French those of Anemones are tearm'd PATTES, and the Fibrous DRAGEONS, but the generall Italian word for all rootes but Bulbes is RADICHE, and for their encreases RADICHETTE. These Ofsetts and other encreases, taken from their Mothers in due seasons, and well planted, will not only prosper, but sometimes produce new flowers quite differing from their parents, and sometimes much exceeding them in beauty, though commonly much alike. But from the SOWING of SEEDS arise wonderfull new Varietys of Flowers, different from their originals in colors, manner of marking, and sometime shape, soe much now and then that the skilfullest Florists cannot guesse at their extractions, for not only double and very large flowers come from the seeds of single and small ones, but Reds & Yellowes out of Whites, and —on the contrary—Whites, Yellowes, Gridelines, and other odde Colours out of Redds, and often flowers with three or fower colours out of such as have only one.

But the Seeds of all kinds are not alike easy to change in this manner; those of Tulipes, Anemones and Beares eares alter most of the best sorts of flowers, espetially if they bee well chosen and gather'd.

OF CHOOSING SEED, and of SOWING and ORDERING it

The best Seed is the most weighty, and is had from the lustiest and most vigorous stemms. Wee use to crop of flowers of such kinds as are many on a stalke, to make the other seede the better and have the more vertue, and such wee finde usually in the Lower Seed vessells of the stalkes. Bee not curious to keep the finest markt Tulipe or other rare flower for seed, unless the kind bee strong, for better flowers are rais'd from a lusty flower of one colour than from a curious strip't one of severall colours that is but weake, and commonly such will hardly afford seede at all.

Gather your Seed in faire weather, and not before it bee full ripe, which you shall perceave by the colour of it, and by the with'ring of the stalke & seedcase, but such seed as rises up with downe, as Anemones and other sorts doe must bee watcht, and taken as soone as the downe rises, which when it is ripe one hour in hot sunshine 'twill doe, if it bee not gather'd presently, and the leaste breath of aire will carry it away.

The Seed of Hardy Annualls is best sowne soone after it is ripe, of Tender Annualls in the Spring, and of all other Flowers from the tyme of their maturity till November (covering them in wynter in frosts) or otherwise from the middle of February till the middle of Aprill, but Autumne is the best season for such.

Some Tender Annualls (such as Amaranthes) will not yet beare good seed in England unless they bee sowne very early in the Spring, and if soe the common way, the cold will nip the budding sprouts that they shall never come to good, therefore there is art to bee used, and much trouble and care, to raise such plants betimes in the yeare in March espetially, which cannot bee done with us but by the means of a hott bed.

Which hott bed is made of a heape of the newest horse dung can bee gott, lay'd three or fower foote high and about a yard broad, of what length you have occasion, cover the top of it with about half a foote thicke of the finest rich sifted mold, then cover it with matts or old blanketts, fower or five dayes & nights together, by which tyme the earth above will bee very hot, then uncover it in the day for three or fower dayes together if it raine not, and as soone as the heate of the mold can bee endur'd by your finger thrust into it, sow or pricke in yr seeds, more or lesse deepe according to their bignes, then cover them up constantly with the clothes or matts untill they begin to sprout, as soone as they appeare give them ayre every day about noone for an hower or two, if it bee fine, but cover them the rest of the day with glasses or matts or clothes, and soe all night and morning supporting yr matts with a frame of wood, or poles that they presse not upon the plants. Keepe them all this tyme from raine or watering as well as you can, and when they have little leaves, transplant them into another dungbed lesse hot that hath serv'd before in this kind, cover them there in the nights and colder parts of the dayes till they are growne strong, and then remove them againe into potts or earth abroad as you please, where you must also cover them with glasses till they are well rooted.

The heate of such a bed as is here described will sett up seedes in a very short tyme, it is also excellent for Indian bulbes to make them shoote out fibres, which they will hardly doe in other places, but care is to bee had that the earth bee not too violent hot when they are put in, and that no moisture considerable come to such rootes before their fibres are strong, otherwise they will certainly rott and die.

But to return to ye Seed, such as are dryed with keeping long, or hot weather, and others that are naturally more contumatious and stubborne must bee steept in warme water or new milke before they bee sowne, and a little incision made with a pen-knife into them to helpe their germination, but hurt not the little spot or point of ye seed, for then it dies.

As your seed must bee gather'd in faire weather, soe it must bee sowed in a dry calme day, in very fine sifted earth, either in boxes, potts or panns, or in bedds. The decrease of the Moone is accounted best to sow in, as the Full to plant rootes, but I think it not materiall to observe either. How ev'ry sort of seed of the choicest flowers is to bee sowne, and when, shall bee said hereafter, speaking particularly of each kind.

OF ARTIFITIALL MULTIPLICATIONS of FLOWERS

Only FIBROUS Flowers can bee Artifitially encreast or Multiplied and that is either by ye old common way of Cuttings and Slips set in the Spring or Autumne in moist, shaded places, as women usually doe Gilliflowers, or by a surer newer way of LAYERS, which are sprigs or branches of flowers (or trees) cut half through a joynt, and soe bowed into the earth in that cut place, and there pin'd fast with a little sticke, and cover'd about the incision with good mold, letting the top of the sprigg stand forth of the earth three or fower inches. And this way is now frequently used with Gilliflowers from Midsomer to September. These layers (of flowers, not trees) will in a moneth's tyme or thereabouts get soe good new rootes about the cut joynt as to bee fit to bee removed and taken of from the old roote, and soe you may in one yeare somtimes have halfe a score new rootes or more from one old stocke, which will better endure the ensuing wynter than their mother.

OF the SEASONS of PLANTING Flowers, and TAKING them up

All sorts of BULBOUS Rootes are best planted from the end of SEPTEMBER to the beginning of NOVEMBER (unless they bee Indian Autumnall flowers) yet sometimes Bulbes set in August, or any tyme in November doe well, but all the other Moneths of Sommer, Spring or Wynter are unfitt for it.

Glandulous follow the rule of the Bulbous, and most Tuberous, but Anemones, espetially those of the hard leafe, are best planted in August, though they may also be set in September, October, November, February & March, and by that meanes bee in flower most parts of the yeare.

But the SPRING is the prime tyme for planting FIBROUS flowers, though Autumne is good also for some, espetially Hepaticas, and such as flower very early in the Spring.

Such Bulbes (whose fibres dye yearly as most doe) are best TAKEN up every yeare, when their leaves and stalkes are well wither'd and the seed ripe, which is commonly the later end of June or beginning of July (except Autumnall plants) but such whose fibres are strong and great, and dye not (as most of the Indian Narcissi and some Hyacynthes & Irises) ought not to bee taken up but in case of necessity, for if they bee long out of the earth those great fibres are dryed and dye, and it is a very hard matter in England to draw out new ones, and without them they cannot grow.

AUTUMNAL Flowers love not removing, but upon occasions take them up just when they have done flow'ring, if they bee of such kinds as put not forth leaves till long after the flowers, if soe, then when the Leaves are well wither'd.

PLANT and DEPLANT all kinds in dry weather, and set no Bulbes in potts, except some Indians which endure not our wynters abroad.

How to KEEPE ROOTES out of the EARTH

The FIBROUS are not to bee soe kept, unles for a short tyme to bee convey'd to other places, and then they must bee still moist, but the Bulbes and Glandulous, as also the Tuberous rootes ought (as hath been said before) to bee a moneth or two at least yearly out of the ground (I meane the choice kinds, for the common may, if you will, stand two or three yeares together in the Earth) and whilst these choice rootes are above ground they must bee kept in a dry roome, but not too close, with such earth sticking to them as came up with them till it fall willingly off, with papers lying with them, or other markes to know them by, or lap't up in papers with their names inscribed, but take heed of ratts, for they will gnaw some sorts, espetially bulbes, and somtimes mice too, if there bee any danger of them then your rootes must be lockt up in boxes, or layd on hanging shelves, that they may bee secur'd from those vermine. And they must not bee heapt too thicke together wheresoever they lye, for soe they will heate and sweat, and then mold, rott and dye. Some keepe their rootes in dry sand, but 'tis not needful if care bee otherwise had as aforesaid.

HOW to PACKE up ROOTES and SEND them to REMOTE PLACES

The FIBROUS sorts must bee made up alone by themselves, with moist mosse or grasse about them tyed fast, which is better than earth, which will dry and fall away, unles the voyage bee short, but all the other kinds must bee packt up dry without earth in papers, and soe boxt up that they shake not, nor have any heavy thing to presse them hard together, and thus they may bee convey'd safely very farr.

How to PRESERVE FLOWERS being PLANTED from HURTFULL things

The worst ENEMYES to gardens are Moles, Catts, Earewiggs, Snailes and Mice, and they must bee carefully destroyed, or all your labor all the year long is lost.

Many storyes there are of pretty wayes to catch Moles, as by putting a pott in the earth with a live Mole in it, to which the rest will resort, and falling in cannot get out againe; by pouring of scalding or poyson'd waters upon their great hills where their nests are and constant dwellings; and diverse others; but I passe them over as fabulous or very little usefull. The only assur'd meanes to destroy them is by watching them heave at sun rising & setting, and then casting them forth with a spade, or striking them with a Mole speare, but I leave this to the direction of the Mole catchers who are everywhere to bee found, and shall rather say somthing of preventing the mischiefes these creatures doe by well walling-in your ground, for if the foundation be anything deepe they cannot get under, for they ever run neare the face of the earth when they are underground, and if the doores shut close at the bottomes, and there bee no holes in the walls, they cannot possibly enter above ground, for they run not up precipices as ratts or mice.

As for Catts they doe much hurt in most places, espetially in Townes if not prevented, for when the earth hath beene lately digged up, as it must bee newly before the planting of your flowers, they delight to scrape in it, and urine and dung upon it. To help which there is no better way than to cover the new planted beds with netts fastned downe close upon them with pinns of wood, which must not bee removed till the earth bee well sadded, and then they are in no great danger.

Earewiggs hurt most Gilliflowers, and are taken best when they are newly podded (for they feed upon the yong pods most) with sheepes hooves stucke upon stickes by the flowers, into which they creepe in the morning to hide themselves all day, feeding all night, and then you shall bee sure of them every morning and may easily kill them.

Snayles doe the leaste harme, and may bee taken in the night in the sommer with a candle as they creepe about, or early in the morning, or after raine.

As for Mice, many grounds are not troubled with them, and where they are they are easily taken with little traps baited with nut kernells, pieces of apples and such things. They are only field mice that trouble the garden, and they hurt most Crocus rootes, being the tenderest and sweetest.

Thus have wee past through some of the chiefest Generall things that were fittest to be knowne before we come to Particulars, and shall say no more, but that all Flowers love to lye soft and dry, soe plant them in due season, and let the beds bee of fine earth, and lye convex, that is somewhat high in the middle, to cast off wett, and let them bee well weeded and kept from the Enemyes, violent weathers, either hot or cold or wyndy, and hurtfull creatures, and your expectation shall bee crown'd with pleasure and delight; for by good cultivation and defence only you shall arrive at the greatest perfection flowers are capable of; for there is no knowne Art to give them such colours as wee desire by steeping the rootes or seedes in colour'd waters, or by putting any ingredients into them that shall worke that effect, nor any way by observing the Moone or heavens to make flowers larger or more double, or to worke such wonders as are both sayd and written to amuse and deceave the unexperienced and credulous.

But now to Particulars, and First of the BULBOUS KINDS whereof the TULIPE is the Chiefe

OF TULIPES

The Tulipe is the Queene of Bulbous plants, whose Flower is beautifull in its figure, and most rich and admirable in colours, and wonderfull in variety of markings.

It is also a hardy plant, and constant enough if well ordered. Wee had it first out of Turkey about fifty yeares since, where it grows wild in some parts, particularly about Jerusalem as they write, and is thought to bee that flower translated ill a Lilly, which was sayd to bee more gloriously array'd than Solomon. The plante is now soe well knowne in England that it needs no description, and therefore wee shall passe that over, as wee shall omit it when we speake of other knowne flowers.

Some kinds of Tulipes blow ever early, that is in the end of March or beginning of Aprill, and we usually call them after the Latine Praecoxes, as the French doe Printanieres, that is Spring Tulipes. These early sorts of Praecoxes are more esteem'd by the curious than the succeeding ones, if they have good colours, and marke well, because they are scarcer than good ones of the later kinds. Some of the best Praecoxes wee have at present of longer standing are Paragon Clermont, the crimson Morillion, Admirall Enchusen, Omen, Oriana, Viceroy and Perushot. Of later yeares the Unique of Delfe, Eugenia, Climene, Clytus, The Venetian, Retrocedee, Dorade, Tamise. Others are of the middle season, which the French call Medionelles, and beginne to bee in flower after the middle of Aprill, and of these there are very many Varietyes.

In the beginning of May the Late sorts blow, of which kind there are but few. These are called in Latine Serotinae, and in French Tardives.

Thus you see the glory of this flower is but short, beginning but at the very conclusion of March, and ending with May, and Art will not force them to blow here at any other season well.

Soe many new sorts of Tulipes have beene rais'd of late yeares in France, and brought hither that it is almost impossible to give a Catologue of the good ones, and the indifferent ones are not without their names too, but I shall set downe some of the best we now possess, first telling you that wee did value in England only such as were well stript with purples and other redds, and pure white; but now, within a yeare or two, we esteeme (as the French doe) any mixtures of odde colours, though there bee no white with them, and such as are markt with any yellowes or Isabellas are much priz'd; all which new colour'd Tulipes wee call Modes, being the fashion, yet new flowers with good Purples or Violets and White are still very deare and valuable.

Of PURPLES *and* VIOLETS *wee have* the Browne purple Marais, other browne purples which commonly have not white enough, Paragon de Acosta rectified, best Brabancons, Cedo nulli, Elisa, Fleuricourt, Generall Picot, Imperiall, Melinda, passe Zabloon, Prince of Wales, Mirandola, Vesta, Amarantine, Celestine, La Vallee, Velouté, Belle Brunne.

Of CRIMSONS *we have* the Generall of Holland, Dorothy of Holland, Paragon of France, Dulcina, Hercules.

Of VIOLETT *colour* the Dorille, Estoilée, Augustine.

Of SCARLETTS, CARNATIONS *and* PINKES Mahomet, Morillion Chirar, Passe Belin, Agat Hanmer, Orientall, Bellincourt, Morine, Rosée.

Of GRIDELINES *and* DOUCE *colours* Carthago, Paragon Hieronimus, Diana, Jaspe Angloise, Nonpareille, Passe Cittadelle, Belle rose, Agat Peruchot, Richmond, Dutches of Venice, and Faustina.

Of NEW MODISH COLORS, or as the French say Bigearre, *wee have* Amidor, deepe red, crimson and yellow; Alquife, browne and yellow; Clytus, much like it but better; Swissesse, also more the same color, but a larger flower; markt like the old Swisse; Erimanthe, hairecolours, red and yellow; Helliodorus, orenge, yellow and crimson; Ignatius, yellow and dead red; Opall, Phoenix, Merlyn, Cupidon, Polonoise, Favourite, Charmante, Supreme, Perseus, Philadelphia, Titania, Passe tout, Zelinde, Clytia, Cleomedon, La Fine, Clelia, La Billy, Agat Bigearre, Belle Bigearre, and diverse others which (as these abovenamed) consist much of hairecolours, and severall yellowes and orenges and brick-colours mixt together with other reds and gridelines.

Most of these and other of our best stript ones come from seed of those of one colour only, which are called SIMPLE OT SINGLE colours, which with age turne from one colour to many (for some Tulipes have fower or five in them) but some single colours are soe stubborne that they will never stripe or pannach (to use the French word) as you may perceave by the old common reds and yellows in our gardens, which never change. Those single colour'd Tulipes that have rich Blew bottomes stripe often in time with White; and those with Greenish bottomes with yellow; the Blacke bottomes seldome stirr or produce any stripings, nor the Yellow.

There are little shaking things standing up like the little heads of speares within the flowers of Tulipes, which the Latine call stamina, and the French Estamyns, and wee Chives and tamines. If these bee yellow the flowers are seldom valuable, being inconstant commonly, and having the colours faint and confused. But if they bee of a rich purple it is almost a certaine signe of a good kind. Soe that such single colours as have purple tamynes are only to bee chosen to gather good seed from, or to keepe in hope of striping well.

It is strange that the great varietyes of stripings and markings come principally from the colours of the bottomes, which are only blew or greenish, and yet when they streame away, as they doe ever wholly in flowers perfected, or rectified (as the tearme is) the leaves retaine not the least blew or yellow in them, but the blew flows into white, and the greene into yellow or colours participating thereof. And it is the more admirable that somtimes the flower changeth soe totally in color that an experienced florist can hardly divine of what stock it is, that is what the simple colour was originally it came from. A flower commonly upon perfecting or rectification becomes lesse, and more tender, and often puts out from the roote a small round rush leafe, pointed at the top, together with the other usuall broad leaves, and somtimes those great leaves are stript or veined with white or yellowish stroakes, but there are some kinds of tulipes which have constantly their great greene leaves border'd or otherwise markt with pure white, very exactly in order and the flowers are nevertheless constantly of one single colour, but there are but few of these.

The finest flowers quickly alter and dye if they bee not cultivated with care and skill, and are small encreasers generally, but being well ordered they retaine their beauty during their lives, and continue as long as the coarser, stronger sorts.

Those with purple chives (as was said before) are most constant to their marking, and goodnes of their colours, and though by reason of unseasonablenes of the yeares they come somtimes ill, yet they become themselves againe the next Spring, if well husbanded.

The BEST propertyes of EARTH for Tulipes are Lightnes and Drynes, yet there must be some saltnes in it. One third part of Sand and two parts of Willow Earth, before spoken of, make an excellent composition for them, but because Willow Earth is not to bee had everywhere take instead thereof two parts of fine, rich, old dry mold out of the fields, or such that is made of leaves

& spriggs, and found about old wood piles, with a little very consum'd cow dung that will passe through a sieve, and adde to them a third part of sand and your rootes will not doe ill. If you can have none of these, then use any old garden mold that is not too moist.

In such Earths as these your Tulipes will flourish, but every two or three yeares at most you must bring in fresh, for they delight in change thereof, as well as of the ayre, soe that your best should not bee long planted in the same beds or places of ye garden, for thereby they will assuredly decay their beautyes.

I know in Paris one of the ablest florists there, who had got a great deal of money by Tulipes, and hee assur'd mee hee chang'd his habitation purposely every third or fowerth yeare in Paris because of his Tulipes, which hee found infinitely better'd by varietyes of aire as well as Earth.

Tulipes must bee planted in Beds abroad and not in Potts, in which they never profit. The Beds should not exceed fower foote in breadth, otherwise they cannot bee well weeded, neither can the middle flowers bee soe well lookt upon in their flourishing season. The Beds ought to lye a little higher in the middle than the sides, that all the flowers may bee seene the better, and espetially that no wett may lye too long about the rootes, which would putrifie them, as the touching of new hott dung will doe to these and all other bulbes. Yet some digg in such deepe under the earth the rootes stand in, the hot fume whereof comforts, as they say, and not destroyes, but I should advise to bee cautious of using it, unles you desire to have yr flowers blow richly one yeare, and never see them blow any more. The greater bearing rootes are to be sett together, and the ofsetts apart by themselves, and consideration is to bee had that in planning your beds with Tulipes you dispose ingeniously of them according to their colours, that there may bee a handsome mixture of them, which will extremely take the eye when they are in flower.

The best way of planting them is after you have made your bed smooth and fine, to draw out soe many little trenches or gutters athwart the bed, as your rootes may stand betwixt halfe a foot and a foot distant from each other, and having set five or six rootes in a gutter or ranke, with the points upwards, to cover them immediately two or three inches over, and soe proceed to the next ranke, writing downe in your Memoriall booke the name of every flower, and how it stands in each ranke, first, second, third, etc. This casting up the Earth in Trenches with your hands, which is easily done with the fine mold, is much better than the making of holes and thrusting the rootes into them, for being not ever fitt, they are somtimes crusht thereby.
Plant in a faire day, and when the Earth is not too wett, for the clammines thereof will bee troublesome, and the bulbes will bee the longer in shooting out fibres if the earthe bee not warme and dry at their setting in.
The best Tyme of planting them is certainly in October, when soever the earth is dry and the weather good, but they who have great store must begin sooner, and may very well in September, as likewise they may safely bee sett in November, but December is commonly too late, espetially for precoxes, and August too early. Those that are planted in November will bee in flower as soone as those set in August.
The beds being planted, and the earth layd very smooth and fine, cover them with netts fastned downe close upon them, if there bee any danger of catts, as there is almost everywhere, and take these not away for a moneth or thereabouts.
You need not water them at all, for about Christmas, if the Frost bee not then great, they will begin to appeare, and soe, in open weather, come up all January and February, and those that have above two leaves will certainly beare that yeare, if they bee not blasted, as those with but one will not assuredly, and such rootes as put forth never a leafe are certainly dead. As soone as ever the Bulbe hath gotten fibres to make it grow,

the flower begins to bee form'd upon its stalke, enveloped in its leaves, in the very middle or belly of it, and then the yong new rootes and ofsetts also begin to come faste to the stalke, all which grow bigg by degrees, and the mother roote perishes yearly without prejudice to its encreases.

In the end of March some Precoxes will bee in flower, and the rest will quickly follow, about the middle of Aprill some Medionelles begin, and in May the late flowerers.

The hott sun will soone dispatch them out of flower, and the Spring stormes of haile and wynds will breake and much hurt them if they bee not shelter'd, and therfore your best beds must have wooden frames to set over them with such little roofes as may support linnen clothes tyed upon them, soe as either side may bee undone and throwne up to looke on the flowers, or to admitt the sun at pleasure, or wholly taken of when you desire to have a full view of them, or the weather is good and temperate. Being thus cover'd they will continue at least a fortnight longer in their beauty than otherwise they would.

And now the Florists fly about to see and examine and take the chiefe pleasure of gardens, admiring the new varietyes that Spring produces, and being impatient of delays open the very buttons scarce yet coloured, but with a little sticke or two for the purpose, lest they should prejudice them with the touch of their fingers.

By the shape and colour of the Leaves and figure of the flower, but espetially by the chives and bottomes wee judge of what kindred or stocke a Tulipe is, and thereby know it, though the colours of the flower and markings change very much some yeares, but those notes are immutable.

When your Tulipes are past flowering, crop off the tops of the stalkes of your choice stript ones, that they may not seed, for thereby they are weaken'd, but keepe for seed such new single colors as are strong, and have good bottomes and chives, and handle not their stalkes much, for that hurts the seed. Let those for seed stand till the seed is full ripe, which is usually in August betimes, and presently you may sow it (and that is best), or any tyme in Autumne or the beginning of the following Spring. Sow in beds abroad, or in potts or other vessells, in fine rich sifted earth, which may stand abroad in the shade in all weathers, covering them with mosse or straw in very hard wynter weather only. They will come up in the Spring (if the seed bee good and new) like to yong onyons or leekes, and must not bee remov'd till the third yeare, but well weeded, and every yeare, in beginning of Spring, have a little very fine rich mold sifted upon them, which will much strengthen and bring them forward.

After the third yeare, remove them yearly till they beare, which commonly will not bee before the fifth yeare. This long expectation makes soe few sow them in England, but in France they make a good trade of it, and their labour and patience is well recompenced, not only with the pleasure of new ones, but the profit, for such that are good sell there at great rates, ordinarily fower or five pounds a roote.

Such rootes as are not for seed are to bee taken up every yeare in the end of June or thereabouts, when the stalkes are wither'd. I meane your best sorts, for the common you may venture to lye still in the earth unremov'd as many yeares as you please, but by no meanes those you value, whatsoever some say to the contrary, for they are subject to more hurt in the earth than out of it, and your garden cannot bee kept handsomely, nor the beds shew full and well unles they bee planted every Spring, otherwise the ofsetts will shoot out irregularly, and there will bee some naked, empty places, for some will dye every yeare, let your care & skill be never soe great.

Being taken up in a dry season, let your rootes bee kept distinctly with their names in paper, or other lead numbers or markes to know them by, in a dry roome on boards, or other shelves or boxes, soe that ratts come not at them till the tyme of their

planting. Before you plant them take away their ofsetts and old skins, and other filth that stickes to them.
This is all necessary to bee said concerning this Noble Flower, which hath beene soe long in Esteeme in Europe, and is like to continue soe. His death proceeds from too much moisture commonly, which is prevented by the sandines of the soils you plant in, but somtimes from a white worme which breeds in the bulbe, and is not to bee destroy'd and the roote preserv'd.

OF NARCISSI, or DAFFODILLS

Wee have many varietyes of Narcissi, but all are of Two Colours only, WHITE *or* YELLOW, *except the Indian kinds.*

Of each of these Colours wee have SINGLE *and* DOWBLE, *some of which beare constantly but one Flower on a stalke, and some two or more, which Florists call after the Greeke word Polyanthes, a name common also to all other flowers that are many on a stalke.*

Of DOWBLE NARCISSI *with* ONLY ONE FLOWER *on a* STALKE, there are *Tradescant,* the greatest dowble Narcissus wee have, of a good yellow color, grows very thicke of leaves, and round like a rose; *Willmers,* or the common dowble yellow, like the former, but not soe round and large.
Dowble Nonpareille, or as they call it in Holland *La Citroniere* which smells very sweete, and is a large flower, with pale lemmon colour'd wings (soe wee call the outward six leaves) and a yellow cup full of small lemmon enfolded leaves growing like a puff, the stalke strong and high. It is a pretty flower and not very common.
Dowble White, it is sweet, and the leaves are pure white, and lye round and orderly. It is common enough in some parts of England. Its greene leaves are of a middle size, not soe large as the former & greater than the next following, which is
Robinus, his Narcissus, soe called from that famous florist of the

name in Paris. It is wholy of a pale lemmon colour, and lyes spread round yet pointed, like the beams of a star. The greene leaves are every way the least of the dowble kinds, and soe is the flower, except those wee call *Jounquilles.*

This last blows commonly about the beginning of Aprill, and the rest in March, except the White, which is later somwhat.

DOWBLE NARCISSI *many on a stalke,* or POLYANTHES, there are *Narcissus Constantinople,* in Latine usually *Bizantinus,* the Flowers are all White commonly, but some have the middle a little yellow or purple. They are very sweet. This is yet well esteem'd, and hath good large greene leaves, but seldome blowes with us unles it stands very warm and in fine earth.

The Dowble Yellow Jounquille with small rush greene leaves. The flower is of a good perfect yellow, and very sweet like Orenge flowers, the roote is small and round and black. These flower in the end of March and beginning of Aprill, if the Spring bee tymely, if not somwhat later.

SINGLE NARCISSI *having but* ONE FLOWER *on a* STALKE. *The Little Early Yellow* which flowers in February. Rush leaved with a long wide mouth'd cup, and very small yellow wings, scarce to bee seene.

The Single Nonpareille, a large flower with pale lemmon wings, and a yellow cup. Common. It smells sweet. The stalke is strong and long, and the leaves large.

The Lady Mattenesse, her Narcissus, lesse than the Nonpareille, yet a faire flower, with wings and cup both yellow.

The Medio Croceus, or white, with a purple edge and saffron cup.

The Great Yellow Spanish, with a very long trunke, all yellow, both wings and trunke.

The Greater All White, with a shorter and lesser trunke than the former *Spanish,* which is the greatest single Narcissus we have.

The White Wing'd daffodill, with the long yellow trunke, a good

faire flower, it blowes late, after all the *Polyanthes*, and *Willmers* and *La Citroniere*. Her greene leaves are short and broad.
The Lesser all White, with the wings hanging downe.
The Common Yellow, with the long trumpe and wings hanging downe, much lesse than ye *Spanish yellow*. It flowers betymes.
The Common White with a little flat pale yellow cup.

All these Flower in March and Aprill.

Alamusco, or the *Virginian* Narcissus, all White, which growes Straight up like a crocus, and hath severall yellow chives within the flower. The greene leaves are narrow and long. It flowers in Aprill & May.
The Mountaine Daffodill, with eares, or as others say in Latine Apophysibus praeditus. The wings are pretty large and white, the cup is yellow and broad. This flowers in May.
The Small Yellow & White turning Jounquilles, or rushleav'd Narcissi. They flower in February and March.
There are two or three Autumnall kinds, bearing one flower only, amongst which is the small *Persian yellow* Narcissus.

SINGLE NARCISSI POLYANTHES, *or with many flowers on a stalke. The Great Yellow Narcissus of Argiers or of Africke*, with large open cupps, very sweet and greater than the single kinds. It beareth many flowers. There is another small sort of this Narcissus with pale yellow cupps & wings & very small flow'rs.
Narcissus Narbonensis, or Donax, or Medio Luteus Precox, the early French Daffodill, with white wings and small yellow cup.

These flower in the end of February & March.

Belle Silvane, the greatest flowers of polyanthes daffodills, with pure white wings, and a small yellow cup. It flowers in the end of March and beares commonly fower or five flowers on a stalke. Well esteem'd, not common.
The All White, with many small flowers, and little cups.

The Italian Medio Luteus, with white wings, and yellow short cups. This is called also the Narcissus of Pisa, the flowers small, five or six on a stalke. It flowers in Aprill.
The Common English with white wings, and small yellow cup. It hath seldome above two or three flowers on a stalke.
Belle del Vigne, the later French daffodill, with a yellow cup.
Musart his Narcissus, spread like a starr, with great pure white wings, and a yellow flat cupp or coronet of a deepe safron color about the brimms.

These flower in March.

There are also severall small narcissi which wee call Jounquilles because of their rush leaves, as

The Snow Jounquille, with the open mouth'd trunke, and soe small wings they are scarce discernable.
The Great White Jounquille, with a lesse cup.
The All White turning Jounquille, that is with the wings turning up to the stalke.
The All Yellow turning Jounquille also with a reasonable long cup as the last hath.

These all flower in the end of March and Aprill.

Besides all these SINGLE POLYANTHES *and some more of lesse note, wee have the*

NARCISSUS TERTIUS MATHIOLI, that is Mathiolus his third Narcissus, a very fine plant, having very large strong leaves standing up stiffely, a strong stalke, with halfe a dozen or more large white flowers of six leaves lyeing spreadd open, with a broad cupp cut into six parts, and not whole as the other cups are, and six white long threads, standing up, crook'd towards the end, tipt with yellow. The rootes very great, almost as bigg as a Squilla, with pereniall Fibers, and the seed great and blacke and round. It springeth not out of the ground untill the beginning of Aprill commonly, and flowreth in the end of May and June.

Thus much concerning all the kinds of Narcissi, which are habituated to ye clime of England. We have besides some INDIAN kinds, which yet take not to live and bear well with us, but the reason, I conceave, is not that they are soe very tender that they cannot endure ye wynters with care over them, but that wee have had but few brought to us as yet, and comming soe farr, the fibers, which are great and pereniall, dry and perish, and are hardly regained here, soe that till we have them brought in greater number wee shall not preserve any. Soe wee have had the experience in severall other plants that have beene severall tymes had out of the Indyes, and failed to grow and like here, yet at length some have hitt, and prosper'd well, and from them wee have had others that have thriven, and done as well as any of our proper European kinds.

I shall describe some of these strangers, and begin with one I had from the Barbadoes in the yeare 1655, which had a longish reasonable large grey roote, which being planted in a pott in the Spring 1656, that May it put forth a great greene smooth hollow stalke, about 2 foote high, without any leafe on it, on the top whereof came two flowers shap't like Lillyes, of a fine shining red color, betwixt an Orenge and a Pinke. In the end of June the flowers were gone, but the stalke continued till after the greene leaves were up, which was in the end of September. They were three in number, of the bignes of ye largest Daffodill leaves, which the frosts of that next wynter kill'd betimes, otherwise they would, I thinke, have continued till Spring.

Three rootes of this kind bore that yeare in three severall gardens in and neere London, but never since, though some of them are yet living, anno 1659, but different from what they did the first yeare, they did put their greene leaves forth of the earth in May, and kept them all the sommer, but no signe of stalke or flowers.

I guesse this to bee an Autumnall bulbe, which bore with us out of its season upon its transportment from the West Indyes hither, being out of the earth when the leaves should have come forth, and it is usuall for bulbes that come from remote parts to beare the first yeare and not afterwards, though the rootes live still, as I have seene often the experience of the flower of Garnsey, as wee call it. Tyme will enforme us better of the reason of these things. Some take this for Narcissus JACOBEUS, but I find severall differences in the descriptions, and till I am more assur'd shall call it Narcissus Barbadicus.

The Sphaericall Indian Narcissus, called also the great Indian Moly, and the Indian Ornithogalum is of great beauty, and rare in England, though it hath beene in France and Italy these twenty yeares. It hath on the top of a high stalke many branches, like those of a brancht candlesticke, the ends whereof turn upwards, and have on each a flower like a lilly, consisting of five leaves, some whereof have their leaves turning downe, and some the contrary, with six chives, and a long middle pointell crooked at the top. The color of the flower is red, like Martagon Pomponium. It flowers in September, and the greene leaves appear then not till November, but if it beare not that yeare then in October, and live till the end of May, if frosts nip them not.

There is another sort of Indian Narcissus, like that of Barbadoes which flowers in September, and hath a greate roote. The flower is as bigg as a white lilly, yellowish at the bottome, with six tamines, whitish below and reddish above, with yellowish greene horned tops. It hath somtimes twenty flowers on a stalke. The leaves appeare not till the flowers are past, and are like our great narcissi leaves.

Another sort of Indian Narcissi is that with onely One Great Flower on a great stalke reddish at the top and spotted below. The flower consists of six leaves of a rich scarlet color like the

Pomegranates, with a multitude of very small red flowers on their little stalks growing like seeds within the great flower, each blossome having three reddish chives tipt with yellowish pendants. It flowers in September, and when it goes to seed, the Greene leaves come up, which are but TWO, short, broad, thicke and of a darke greene colour.

Cornutus describes two other Indians thus. The first is a Dwarfe kind, with many red flowers upon one flat stalke, of the shape and bignes of the Meadow Colchicum, consisting of six leaves apiece, and six chives with blew tips. The flower is extreame sweet as well as beautifull. The Roote is great and fleshy, the greene leaves are eight or nine, a palme long, and an inch broad. They grow winding upon the ground, and come forth of the ground together with the naked flower stalke, which the other Indian kinds doe not. This is in flower Ante Arcturum, and passes away in eight dayes in ye Northerne countreys without seed. This must needs bee the same with the Figure in Parkinson which hee describeth not, but onely calleth it Narcissus marinus exoticus, a strange sea daffodill, and soe leaveth it.
The second described by Cornutus is by him called Narcissus Japonicus rutiloflore, the narcissus of Japan with the red flower. The stalke (hee sayth) is naked, a foote high, greene above, but spotted with browne spotts beneath, on the top whereof, on little footstalkes stand nine or ten bright red flowers, of six leaves apiece, two inches long, but narrow, with a little furrow or crease in the middle, the leaves turn a little downe at the ends like Martagons. The chives are six, longer than the leaves of the flowers, and paler red, with purple tips. It hath no smell at all. The leaves are not great, of a pleasant greene colour, they come not forth till the stalke is wither'd.
It flowred the seaventh day of October 1634 in Morynes garden in Paris.

All or most of the Indian Narcissi have pereniall fibers, that is such as live all the yeare, and are Hermafroditicall plants partaking of two Speties, viz. the Lilly and the Narcissus, to the first they resemble in the shape of their flowers, and to the latter in their rootes, greene leaves, and some other particulars. The observ'd constant differences betwixt the Lilly and Narcissus are fower. 1. The Lilly hath commonly a scaly or rough Bulbous roote, the Narcissus a smoothe one. 2. The Lilly stalkes are ever beset with small leaves from the bottomes to the tops, but the Narcissi have none at all. 3. The Lilly leaves come up a good while before the stalke and flowers, which those of the Narcissi doe not. 4. The Flowers of the Narcissi breake forth out of a membraneous skin, which the Lillyes doe not, but only out of a greene pod.

Besides all the abovementioned Narcissi there is a sort called PANCRATIUM, which is the Sea Daffodill, one of which hath White Flowers and is somtimes called in Latine Hemerocallis Valentina Clusy, and the other hath Red Flowers and is called PANCRATIUM MAIUS HISPANICUM. They both flower in Autumne, and have very great rootes and broad leaves.

All ye Narcissi are easily preserv'd with us in a good mold, soe it bee not very wett. Every third yeare they ought to bee taken up to free them from their ofsetts, which doe encrease very much with most kinds. The season for that is in July, when their stalkes are fully wither'd; they must not bee left longer for they quickly shoot out new fibres, and then 'tis ill removing 'em. They may bee kept out of the earth till about Michaelmas, and then 'tis best replanting them, though any tyme in Autumne may serve the turne.

The Indian Narcissi and the Pancratia are very tender, and difficultly preserv'd. They must bee put into vessells that bee hous'd in wynter. They ought to be set at first in a sandy mold in Spring, with consum'd dung, in potts in a hott bed to draw out the fibers, and then remov'd, pott and all, to stande under a warme wall, where they must bee coverd with glasses in the nights, and cold stormy days.

Water not the rootes before they grow apparently, and if they take to grow, remove them not, but put new mold of sifted dung and earth to the rootes yearly as they stand. Take them not forth of the house from October to the middle of Aprill.

The Indians come not here to that perfection as to afford seed, neither doe any of the Dowble kinds yield any. The other sorts doe most of them seed well, which if gather'd full ripe, and in faire weather, and sowed in fine, small, rich mold in potts, or otherwise, will produce encrease enough, but seldome any new kinds.

Thus much concerning Narcissi or Daffodills, to which wee will only adde this note, that those are called Bastard Narcissi, or according to Latine authors PSEUDONARCISSI, which have their cupps or trunkes longer than their wings, or leaves of their flowers, and those with the very short cups or coronetts are the true Narcissi.

OF HYACINTHS, or JACYNTHS

Wee have fower kinds of Bulbous Hyacinths, which differ most in their flowers, though a little also in their leaves and Bulbes. The first and chiefe in esteeme are the TRUE HYACINTHS, *of which there are many sorts, differing most in colour, but somwhat too in the greatnes of the flowers and number of them. The flowers are ever many on a stalke, shapt like little bells, but devided or snipt on the edges or mouths, and of these our common English flower, which in many countreys of England they call a Harebell is one sort. There is another sort which wee call* STAR HYACINTHS *the flowers whereof are not soe long as the former, but are spread open like little starrs, with little threads or chives, and six pointed leaves. The third sort is the* GRAPE HYACINTH, *in Latine Hyacinthus Botryodes, or the bottle hyacinth, because the flowers are like little juggs or bottles with open mouths, and are many together on the tops of the stalkes like little bunches of grapes. Fourthly*

HAIRY HYACINTHS, *whose flowers are winding haires or threads, or little bushy haires in tufts on the tops of the small bottle flowers.*

OF THE TRUE OR PROPER HYACINTHS

There are great diversityes of these as I have already sayd, differing in color, greatnes, and seasons of bearing. The fairest and largest we call ORIENTALL, because they came first out of Turkey, and the Eastern countreys, whereof there are some Blew, pale and deepe, smelling sweet, and some White, all which flower betimes, and some of the same colors which flower later, amongst which the rarest is the DOWBLE WHITE, and the Flesh color, and the Ash color. And after all these come the Violet color polyanthes, single and dowble, the sweet pale Watchet, called in Haly Januarius, from a Gardiner's name, and the dowble Sky or Blew, called there Roseus, from the figure like a rose blowne, and the Rosemary color.

These flower in March or Aprill, and have their seed ripe in the end of May, and beginning of June in England. Their greene leaves come up in December and January.

After these Orientall sorts, we esteeme two smaller sorts, that is the English and the Spanish.
The English are single, of WHITE, BLEW and BLUSH colours. They flower in Aprill.
The Spanish are the BLEW, the RED and the DUNNE, or a sad white color. They flower in May.
Besides all these there is a sort of the true Hyacinths which hath a Lilly leafe, and a strong stalke spotted with red, and large BLEW flowers. It beares in Aprill.

OF STARR HYACINTHS

We have the small early WHITE & BLEW, which flower in February.

The WHITE
The VIOLET } which flower in Aprill.
The BLUSH
The great BLEW of CONSTANTINOPLE.
The Branch'd HYACINTHS of PERU, of which these three sorts, the Rich BLEW, the WHITE and the BLUSH color, very rare here. The leaves of these are shorter, and of a darker greene color than the former. They beare in the beginning of May.
There is also a late Blew Starr Hyacinth with a scaly roote, and another BLEW and an AUTUMNALL WHITE.

OF GRAPE, or BOTTLE HYACINTHS

Wee have the pale yellow sweet MUSCARI, and the ASH colour'd MUSCARI, which flower in March and Aprill, and are not common.
And the Common small WHITE, the RED and the BLEW, which flower a little after the Muscari.

OF HAIRY HYACINTHS

Wee have HYACINTHUS COMOSUS, which hath a hairy tuft comes forth of the top flowers of the stalke, which flowers are either purple or white (a dead white).
And HYACINTHUS COMOSUS RACEMOSUS, the branched hairy hyacinth, the ends of every branch winding and turning with brittle red-purple threads or haires instead of flowers. This kind is often called Hyacinthus SANNESIUS. They both flourish in May.

A good garden mold that is not wet, and hath no new dung in it agrees well with all Hyacinths. They love a warme place, but live well abroad all wynter, and must bee as seldome remov'd, and as little out of the ground as may bee. The Season to take them up is in the end of June or beginning of July, and to replant them in September, and if need bee in October or November.

Sow the Seed in September in fine mold, as is directed for Tulipes, let them stand abroad in the shade, and water them somtimes with a fine water pott. Remove the yong rootes the second or thirde yeare, as they prosper in bignes.

OF BULBOUS IRISES

There are Two Sorts of BULBOUS IRISES, *the* GREAT *or* LATIFOLIAS, *because they have broader leaves than the other, and are stronger plants.*
The LESSER *or* ANGUSTIFOLIAS, *after the Latine word, because they have narrower greene leaves, and have smaller rootes and flowers than the former.*
Of the GREAT SORT *wee have but a few in comparison of the other, and they are generally by writers called English Irises, as if they were most of them naturall to our country, but I have not knowne any of them grow wild or naturally in England as some of the Flag-leav'd doe. They have a little pale yellow spot on their three falling leaves, and grow commonly with two flowers on every stalke.*

GREAT BULBOUS IRISES

These following are all the varietyes I have seene:
CLUSIUS his FIRST IRIS, soe called from him that described it first and because hee treats of it first in his booke. It is commonly of a pale BLEW colour, but somtimes WHITE is to bee found. It is also called IRIS LUSITANICA LATIFOLIA, the broad leav'd Portugall Iris. It flowers first of any Iris in the Spring, in January commonly.
The PERSIAN Iris, whose falls or falling leaves are of a shining MURREY or deepe purple, like velvet, and the standards of a very pale WATCHET. It flowers betimes in February.
L'ABBÉ, in English the Abbot's Iris, all wholy of a fine pleasant PURPLE colour, excepting the Yellow spot which all Irises have, deeper or paler. The leafe of this is very narrow.
The CHINA or Porcelain Iris, markt like a porcelane dish, with a delicate BLEW upon a pure WHITE.

These two last blow not till May, and all the fower abovementioned have lesser flowers and leaves than those Latifolias following, though greater than the Narrow leaved.

The GREAT PURPLE, all of that color.
The DEEPE BLEW, all of that color.
The DEEPE BLEW spotted with DEEPE MURREY, called by some the CHAMLET Iris.
The PALE BLEW, or IRIS CELESTIS.
The LAVENDER, or ASH colour.
The WHITE, of which there are two sorts, but the difference is not great.
The PEACH, which is the White markt with some Peach color.

These seaven sorts put forth greene leaves in the end of January & February, and Flowers in the end of May and beginning of June.

SMALL BULBOUS IRISES

There are of late tyme abundance of this sort, many of which have beene rais'd from seed in France, and have had names impos'd upon them. Monsieur Moryn, a famous Florist in France, hath printed a Catalogue in French of above three score severall sorts, which hee had growing in his garden in Paris about two years since, whereof wee have many now in England. Hee names and describes them thus, calling the three falling leaves Falls, the three leaves which stand up Standards or Sayles somtimes, and the little tongues or short leaves lying on the Falls Arches.

The Agat Iris, with grey and violet standards, and yellow and umber falls.
The African, with yellow and blew falls, violet standards, and pale yellow arches.
The Aleppo Iris, with yellow falls, and all the rest yellow and a durty white.

The Iris of Amboise, with yellow falls, yellow and blew arches, and pale grideline standards.
The Iris of the Antients, with white falls border'd with pale blew, the rest all blew. It flowers late & smells sweet.
The Iris of Arabia, with golden falls, smoaky haire color arches, and violet standards.
The Iris of Auvergne, with yellow and blew falls, blew arches, and violet standards markt with blew and haire colour.
The Iris du Bois, with pale yellow falls, and whitish blew standards; it is a dwarfe and like the Iris of Castile.
The Iris of Blois, with Aurora falls, yellow and blew arches, and grideline and aurora standards.
The Iris of Boulogne, all of a whitish brimstone.
The Iris of Brittany, with yellow falls and arches, and faded white standards.
The Iris of Bry, with yellow falls, white and yellow arches, and white and blew standards.
The Camolote Iris, with yellow and haire color falls, deare colour arches, quoist color standards, when it pannaches is called Moryne's Iris.
The Iris of Candy, with yellowish olive falls and arches, and grideline standards.
The Iris of Castile, with yellow falls and the rest durty white.
The Damaskt Iris, is white pannach't with violet; this comes from the Iris of Portugal.
The Iris of Egypt hath blew falls and arches, and violet standards.
The Iris of Florence, all white, a little flower.
The Iris of Florida, with blewish falls, and violet standards mixt with grideline.
The Iris of the Frontiers, with blew and yellow falls, and violet standards.
The Iris of the Furillants, with haire color falls, deare colour arches, and quoist colour standards.

The Iris of Gascony, with peach color falls and arches, and pale blew standards.
The Iris of the Grand Signior, with yellow falls border'd with haire color, and grideline arches and standards.
The Iris of Greece, with blew falls and arches, mixt with a little yellow, and violet and white standards.
The Iris of Guynea, with haire color falls, pale blew arches, and violet standards.
The Iris of the Indyes, with yellow falls and arches, and grideline and violet standards.
The Iris of Judea, with yellow and blew falls, the rest deepe violet.
The Iris of the Levant, with Isabella and umber falls, light blew arches, and blew and white standards.
The Iris of the Lombards, with white falls and arches, and blew standards.
The Iris of Lorraine, with white falls, the rest all pale blew.
The Iris of Libya, with yellow falls, the rest mixt yellow.
The Iris of Macedonia, with the falls and arches aurora and yellow, the standards quoist color, or the colour of a ringdove's breast.
The Iris of the Maldines, with straw color falls, pale yellow arches mixt with blew, lively blew standards mixt with yellow.
The Iris of Melinda, all of the colour of a Pansy.
The Iris of Mexico, with yellow falls, yellow and blew arches, and grideline and violet standards.
The Iris of Millan, with light blew falls, and arches, and grideline standards.
The Iris of the Moluccaes, with yellow and aurora falls, lemmon and blew arches, and blew standards with violet bottomes.
The Orientall Iris, with violet and yellow falls, violet arches, and violet and purple standards.
The Perfect Iris, with reddish violet and purple falls, the arches mixt violet, the standards lively violet.

The Iris of Parma, all violet, but more beautifull and rare than that of Portugall, which is also all violet.

The Iris of Picardy, with haire color and smoaky blew falls, smoaky haire color arches, purple, dove colour, and some haire color standards.

The Iris of the Poetts, with olive greene and blew falls, and the rest blew.

The Iris of Poictou, with yellow falls and arches, and haire color standards.

The Iris of Portugall, all violet; this is an early one.

The Iris of Puy, with yellow and umber falls, blew arches, mixt with umber, and violet standards.

The Pirenean Iris, with yellow falls, yellow and blew arches, and light blew standards.

The Rochtaine Iris, with yellow falls and arches, and grideline standards.

The Royall Iris, with light haire color and umber falls, dirty haire color and blew arches.

The Iris of Savoy, with aurora falls, smoaky yellow arches, and haire color standards.

The Iris of Sicily, all yellow, but lesse than that of Calabria.

The Iris of Siena, all yellow, like that of Calabria, but beares more flowers.

The Swisse, with yellow falls, the rest blew and yellow.

The Iris of Syria, with umber falls, ye rest light blew.

The Iris of Tartary, with pale yellow mixt falls, and fowle blew standards.

The Turkey Iris, with bright minimme color falls, and haire color arches and violet standards.

The Iris of the Valleys, with blew and haire color falls, blewish arches, and violet standards.

The Iris of Valois, with yellow falls, mixt yellow arches, and durty grideline standards, stript all along with yellow, like ye Iris of Blois.

The Iris of the Vaudois, all blew, it beareth somtimes a dozen or more flowers.
The Venetian Iris, hath blew and white falls, blew arches and violet standards.

All these and other of the small bulbous kinds flower in the end of May and June, and their seed is ripe in the end of August.

All Bulbous Irises have their standards much lesse than their falling leaves, and the Tuberous the contrary ever.
They love a reasonable loose mold, somwhat sandy, and rot presently if new dung come to the rootes.
It is better to let them stand two or three yeares than to take them up yearly, and it is not good to keepe them long out of the earth, but they may without great hurt bee kept as long as Tulipes unsett. The tyme to take them up is when the stalkes are well wither'd, and to replant them any tyme from Michelmas or beginning of September to Christmas, or very neare.
The SEED is to bee sowed and ordered as Tulipe seed, that of the lesser sorte of bulbous Irises produces often new kinds, but the striping comes commonly with age, as it does to Tulipes.
In fower yeares your seed will bring flowers.
There needs no more to bee sayd of them, but that they are all hardy enough, prospering better abroad in the full earth with us than in potts, and in the shade than too hot a sun.
They all encrease exceedingly in offsetts, if they like the ground.

OF CROCUSSES

Crocusses are either of the Autumne or Spring.

Autumnall Crocuses are the True Crocus that beares the Saffron, which is of a grideline color, and is called in Latine Crocus verus sativus purpureus; or the Silver coloured, called also Byzantinus, or of Constantinople.

The first is in flower in September and the other in October.

Spring Crocusses, wee have the WHITE, of which there are severall sorts, but one with a great blew bottome.
The GRIDELINE or Purple, whereof some are deeper coloured, some paler, and some have larger flowers, as others lesse, and some are stript, but the colours passe not through of all sorts.
The best is that wee call WALKER'S CROCUS, equally markt with stripes of pure white, and purple or grideline, which passe perfectly.
The GOLD YELLOW, and the yellow stript on the outward leaves with a deepe Murrey.

The Spring kinds flower in January and February, and come up with their flowers a little before their small greene leaves. The stript yellow is one of the first in flower, and the pure white last. They all love a fine garden mold, to bee seldome remov'd, and little out of the earth. The rootes are naked, yet endure the wynter colds abroad in ye gardens very well. The field mice doe often eat the rootes in the ground, and therefore must bee taken in traps or otherwise destroyed, with poyson'd kernells or apples. The seed produces little novelty, but the rootes encrease exceedingly in a good earth.

OF COLCHICUMS, or MEADOW SAFFRANS

The Colchicum was soe called (as writers affirme) from the Graecian Island, Colchos. The flower is very like to the Crocus, but 'tis larger, and the roote much bigger and more pointed. The seed is round and brownish coloured. The greene leaves, which come not up till the flower is past, and of most sorts not till Spring, are smooth, larger, and long, like to those of the Lilly generally, but some of the chequer'd kinds have shorter and darker greene leaves.
They are, as Crocusses, of Two Seasons, the Spring & Autumne.

Of the SPRING I know none but one, with a grideline flower, which blows betymes in February.

AUTUMNALL COLCHICUMS *wee have*

The White, with many flowers, called in Latine Pannonicus.
The Yellow.
The Chequer'd Purple of Constantinople, with many flowers, and leaves as broad as the Hellebore.
The Chequer'd Purple of Portugall, an early sort, almost as large as that of Constantinople.
The Chequer'd Purple of Naples (or Fritillaricum, as Latine authors call it) with a great flower, and strong apparent markes.
The Chios Colchicum, chequer'd also, the flower is lesse than the other chequer'd sorts, but neatly markt in squares with two purple colours, which quickly spreade wide open. It is an early one, flowering in the beginning of Autumne, and the leaves are very short, winding & darke greene.
The Single Purple, or pale Grideline, markt with white.
The Dowble of the same colour and markes.
The Small Mountaine Spanish of a purple color.

These begin to flower in September, and continue in succession all Autumne.
They all love a good soyle, and a warme station abroad, but are not to bee hous'd in wynter. They may bee taken up when their greene leaves are wither'd, and yet againe in August and September, ye later sorts may bee kept longer unplanted if need bee.

OF LILLYES

Martagons are usually called by writers Mountaine Lillyes, but wee shall speake of them hereafter, now of those that are commonly called LILLYES, *whereof there are two kinds. The one hath the flowers* ERECT, *or standing up on the stalke, and the other its flowers* PENDULOUS, *or hanging downe.*

Of the Pendulous wee have only the PERSIAN LILLY, which hath a long stalke, besett with long narrow leaves, and many flowers

of a dead or worne purple color, consisting of six leaves apiece, with a long pointell, and chives tipt with yellow. The seed is flat, and like the browne Imperialls, but lesse, as the roote is also, and is not soe much skaled as the other Lillyes.
It flowers in Aprill or May.

Of Erect Lillyes, we have the COMMON SINGLE WHITE, and the DOWBLE WHITE, which seldome opens well with us, and is therefore worth little. The SINGLE DEEPE RED OR BLOODY LILLY, and the same DOWBLE, the RED with bulbes on the stalkes, and the ORENGE or yellowish red.
These Erect Lillyes are all in Flower in JUNE OR JULY. They all thrive well in any good garden mold, and endure the wynters abroad without any care of them, and may stand either in a shady or hot place. The lesse the rootes are forth of the earth the better, but if they bee remov'd the best tyme is July, presently after they have done bearing, for they begin quickly after to shoot out new fibers. The greene leaves come up in Autumne, and abide all wynter, and till the flowers are also past.
The seed of all Lillyes is flat, reddish and cartilageous, which is seldome sowne, because it produces little variety.

OF MARTAGONS

These are a kind of Lillyes, and therefore may fitly bee placed here, the Latine writers call them usually Lilia Montana. They are of TWO SORTS, *either with* NARROW LEAVES *or* BROAD. *The narrow greene leaves grow dispersedly upon the stalkes, from the bottomes to the tops, but the broader by ascents or degrees in roundlets encompassing it.*

Of the BROAD LEAV'D Martagons *wee have*

The IMPERIALL with very many pale flesh colour'd flowers, spotted with rusty spotts, with yellow chives tipt with red. The greene leaves come up about the beginning of March.
The WHITE, comes somwhat later than the Imperiall.

The White spotted with ORENGE.
The LIGHT RED called Martagon Pannonicum, which I have not seene, ergo quaere.

These flower in June or beginning of July, and spring up in February.
There is said to bee another sort, which is Yellow spotted with browne spotts, having large leaves growing in Roundlets by degrees on the stalkes as the former, but not having seene it I passe it over. It is by writers called the Martagon, or Lilly of Canada in the West Indyes.

Of NARROW LEAV'D MARTAGONS *wee have*

POMPONIUM, which beares flowers plentifully, of a fine red colour like Red Wax, this is a Praecox, as soone in flower as any of the rest, and is beautifull and not very common.
The PALE YELLOW, with red chives, early like Pomponium.
The DEEPER YELLOW comes a little later than the last, and hath larger flowers, which endure the wett better than the last.
The GREENISH YELLOW, spotted with darke browne spotts.
The RED VIRGINIA spotted with browne spotts, the greene leaves come up in the beginning of Aprill. This is yet scarce to bee had.
The YELLOW VIRGINIAN, scarcer than ye last.
The RED of CONSTANTINOPLE, very common in England, latest in flower.

These flower all in the end of May & June, & some yeares in July.

All the sorts but the Virginians are very hardy, and those will in tyme bee soe too, but yet wee pott and house them commonly. They all love a good rich earth and not wett, and (as all skaly rootes) endure not to bee long kept out of the earth, but the tyme to take them up is presently after their bearing, which is in the end of June for most kinds, for they quickly shoote out new fibers, and then 'tis naught stirring them.

The seed is flat and browne like a Lillyes seed, but lesse. Wee seldome sow it because it varyes not much, and the encreases from the rootes are great.

OF CROWN IMPERIALLS

which have very great rootes, yellow of color, and smelling strong like a fox. Their greene leaves come up in February, their seed is like a Lillyes seed but greater, they grow without trouble in any good garden mold.

The SORTS *of them are only* THREE, *which are*

The ORDINARY SINGLE ORENGE, of an ill dead orenge color.

The DOWBLE ORENGE, yet rare.

The SINGLE YELLOW, more rare.

The flowers hang downe at the top of the stalke under a tuft of greene leaves. They consist of six leaves, with six chives, and a long fork'd pointell.

They flower in March and Aprill, and are kept and encreas'd without difficulty in our gardens abroad all the yeare.

OF GLADIOLI, or CORN FLAGGS

Wee have three sorts reasonable common in England, which are the CRIMSON, *which is the commonest of all, and runs presently over a garden with its spreading rootes, the* BLUSH *or* FLESH *colour, and the* WHITE.

All which have flowers only on one side of the stalke, and beare in MAY.

Two other sorts, which are the BEST & LARGEST are rare, espetially the last; they are that of Constantinople, with great CRIMSON flowers, sett on both sides of the stalke, which flowers also in May; and the Aethiopian, described first by Cornutus, which was brought from the Cape of Good Hope in Africa, it hath a very great netted bulbous roote, and broad long leaves, and light RED towards SCARLET Flowers, growing on both sides of the stalke. It is said to flower in October.

All the kinds which wee have in England, which are all those abovementioned, except the Aethiopian, prosper well abroad in our gardens, in a blacke loose mold, all wynter, and are only us'd to bee encreased by their yong rootes.
They are not taken up yearly, but to bee remov'd when they encrease too much, and to bee kept but a little tyme out of the earth.
The Flowers are long and gaping, in shape very like to Fox-gloves, each flower upheld by a greene leafe. The seed is reddish & flat, somwhat like that of ye Fritillary.

OF ORCHISES

There are many sorts of Orchises, whose rootes differ little, for every kind hath two bulbes like testicles, about the bignes of small olives, one of which is every yeare full and vegetative, and alternately wrinkled, flaccid, and in a manner wither'd & dead. In this plant Nature seems to sport, imitating in its flowers the shapes of severall creatures, as beasts, birds, flyes, and even Man himselfe too, and from their resemblances the severall sorts are denominated.

Some of the principall are these:

The Ape or Monkey Orchis, called in Latine (but after the Greeke) Orchis Cercopithecophora.
The Lizard Orchis, Scincophora, or Saurodes, this hath longer narrower leaves than the rest.
The Butterfly Orchis, Psychodes, it is called by writers Dyphylla, because it hath but two greene leaves like a Lilly, not spotted with red spotts as the other sorts are.
The Fly Orchis, Myodes, very good in and about Cambridge.

The Bee Orchis, Orchis Melitias.
The Gnat Orchis, Specodes.
The Spider Orchys. Andrachnitis.
The Bird Orchys, Ornithophora, or Orchis Serapias secunda minor Dodonaei. The leaves are like those of the common Hellebore.
The Man Orchis, of two sorts, Male and Female. The flowers are purple before they blow, and of a fine flesh color after, besprinkled as it were with gold dust. This is rare, yet sayd to bee found lately neare Oxford. It was found long since in the woods in Italy, and described by Ferrarius.

There are other kinds of Orchises called Spirales in Latine, which smell well, and their names are Tetrorchis major and minor, as also there is Morio maior et faemina, but these are not soe much esteem'd as the former kinds.
Most of these bulbous orchises are in flower in Aprill & May.

There is another kind called Orchides Palmata, because their rootes are like hands brancht out into fingers, but of these amongst the Tuberous plants.

The bulbous kinds love a good rich soyle, and the shade, and to bee seldome remov'd, and kept little out of the earth, but when there is cause transplant them in September or quickly after, if from the fields, take them up as you find them in flower, with a good clod of earth about their rootes.

OF ORNITHOGALUMS

There are three kinds of this plant that are larger, both in the roote and flowers, and have more flowers on them than the other sorts, and therfore are more esteem'd, of which

The ARABIAN Ornithogalum is the rarest as it is the tenderest. The flowers are pure white, with a black button or shining head in the midst, with six white chives tipt with yellow about it. They are somwhat like to the greatest starr Hyacinth flowers, but larger. Every flower stands on a footstalke of its own, & closes every night, at the bottome of it is a little greene leaf. It smells faintly sweete, and is often called by writers the Lilly of Alexandria. It flowers in JUNE.

The next in beauty to the Arabian is the GREAT WHITE SPIKED Ornithogalum, by some called the ITALIAN Ornithogalum. This kind hath many pure white flowers on a stalke, which blow by degrees from the bottome of the stalke upwards. They are like the flowers of starr hyacinths, and their greene leaves resemble those of the greatest Orientall Hyacinths. These come up in January, and continue till the stalke with the blossomes appeares. In the midst of these flowers there is a white head, besett with many white threads. The seed is round and blacke, and the roote very broad and flat at the bottome, as all those of the other sorts are.

There is another sort of Spiked White Ornithogalums described by Ferrarius, and called by him Peregrinum, which differs from this last in that the greene leaves of this Peregrinum are shorter like to the Peru Hyacinthes, and lye on the ground, whereas the leaves of the other sorts stand up, and the flowers of this are blowne all together, whereas the lowermost of the other dye before the higher come forth. These flowers are like to the White Syringaes, & have in the middle a greenish head, which in tyme turnes whitish, and the roote is as bigg as that of Arabia.

There is also a sort of WHITE Spiked Ornithogalum, whose flowers are streak'd with greene on their backes, which makes the greatest difference.

Then wee have the NAPLES or Neapolitan Ornithogalum, whose flowers are white within, and greenish yellow without. Instead of a head in the middle of the flowers (as most ornithogalums have) this hath another little flower, with white chives tipt with yellow.

The HUNGARIAN OR PANNONICUM, as it is called in Latine, which hath WHITE flowers also, streakt with greene on the backes, but larger than our Starrs of Bethlem. The greene leaves of this kind come up before wynter, which those of the other kinds doe not.

The smaller and lesse esteem'd Ornithogalums are the STAR of Bethlem, with white flowers stript with greene on the backes; the little WHITE, with one leaf; the Early YELLOW, which flowers in the end of March.

But all the Great Sorts flower in APRILL and MAY.

The Arabian kind is, as I sayd, tender, and therefore rare with us, yet it may bee preserv'd, either abroad, under a warme wall, in a pott, or hous'd in wynter. It is very beautifull. The other sorts require also a good warme place, and good fine mold, and to bee seldome remov'd, but the best tyme to take them up is the end of July.

OF THE DENS CANINUS, or Dogg tooth'd Violet

This plant hath a short broad greene leafe, much bespotted with a red colour, like the Orchises. They shew themselves usually in January, and are ever two in number, and quickly lye along on the earth. The roote is a small long bulbe, commonly bending crooked towards the top. The flower is but one on the stalke, and is very like in shape to a little Lilly, or rather a Martagon, because the flowers hang downe, and turne a little backe, and have long seeds on chives, and a pointell. The seed is yellowish and small.

There are but two sorts that I have seene, which are

The WHITE flower'd, whose greene leaves are narrower and longer than the others are, and the light PURPLE OR FLESH colour. Both flower in March. They love a rich earth and a warme place, and endure not to bee long out of the ground.

OF BULBOUS VIOLETS

Wee have these kinds

The EARLY WHITE, whose pretty pure white bellflowers are tipt with a fine greene, and hang downe their heads. It blows in February & March.
The LATER WHITE, which is like the former, but a stronger plant, and blows in May.
The AUTUMNALL, a very small one, otherwise like the others.

In Gerard there are two other sorts mentioned which I have not seene, the one called the Early one of Constantinople, in Latine Leucoium precox Bizantinum. It is sayd to beare a white flower as bigg againe as the other sorts, in September, and the other is sayd to be blew by Lobel, and is called Leucoium Triphyllum flore caeruleo, the three leav'd blew bulbous violet.

All the sorts wee are acquainted with are very hardy, and prosper well abroad in a good garden mold. The season of taking them up, which should bee but seldome, is just as soone as their greene leaves are wither'd well.

OF MOLYES, or Wild Garlicks

The Chief sorts are

HOMER'S PURPLE MOLY, or Theophrastus, his Moly. It hath a broad Lilly leafe, and many starr flowers standing on the top of a strong naked stalke. It beareth little bulbes on the stalke and leaves, which will take roote being planted.
HOMER'S WHITE MOLY, differing from the former only in the colour of the flowers.
They are in flower in June.
The BROAD LEAV'D YELLOW Moly, with two leaves like Tulipe leaves. It beares in May.
The BROAD LEAV'D INDIAN Moly, with a head or cluster of greene bulbes instead of flowers. The leafe is as large as the Hellebores, and the roote very great.

It beares in June.
The GREAT INDIAN PURPLE Moly, with long broad leaves, flowers in June also.
URSIN's Moly, with white flowers, and good large leaves.
The PURPLE NEAPOLITANE Moly.
These last two flower in June & July.
The SWEETE OR MUSKE Moly, with white flowers. This hath a much lesser roote than the former sorts (no bigger than a nut) and small rush leaves, and beares late in the yeare, but is added here because of the difference in its smell from the former, and all other Molyes, this smelling very sweet, almost like Civet, and the rest strong of Garlicke.

There are severall other small sorts of Mountaine Molyes, with purplish or whitish flowers, which are here omitted as of little beauty.
All the Molyes prosper well abroad all wynter, in good mold in our gardens, and yield good seed, which is small and blacke, something resembling that of Gilliflowers. They may bee kept out of the earth as Garlicke is, and planted about Michelmas or after.

OF FRITILLARIES

The roote is a little naked flat white bulbe, with a gaping cleft in the middle, from whence the stalke shoots out, which is long, small and tough, here and there besett with small, long, narrow leaves. The Flowers are of the shape of bells, and hang downe from the tops of the stalkes, as the Crown Imperialls doe. We have severall varietyes of them, as

The Early Chequer'd Purple, which is common.
The Greater Purple, later.
A Blacke Deepe Purple.
A White with one or two, and another with more flowers.
A Pale Yellow, whose flower is longer and smaller than the other. It is not common. It lies a good while on the ground before the stalke & flower stand up. [It came up in Feb. 1660.]

A Yellow Spotted.
A Greenish Yellow.
A Bright Red, towards a Carnation.
The Little Blacke Pyrenean, called the blacke fritillary.
The Spanish Darke Murrey, bearing many flowers at the top, and shorter, broader leaves than the other sorts. [It came up with mee 1660 in the end of January.]

All but the first and the last flower in Aprill.
They must stand warme, and bee out of the earth but a very short tyme.

OF TUBEROUS PLANTS

Having ended the Bulbous Flowers wee are now, according to our Method come to the TUBEROUS, *amongst which I conceave the pre-eminence due to the* ANEMONE, *as being the plant amongst them of the greatest beauty and varietyes.*

OF ANEMONES

There are three kinds of Anemones. 1. *The Broad or Hard leav'd, in Latine Latifoliaes.* 2. *The Small or Soft leav'd, in Latine Tenuifoliaes.* 3. *The Hermaphrodites, whose leaves are like to the Tenuifoliaes, and their flowers most like the Latifoliaes.*

Of Hard or Great Leav'd Anemones, in Latine Latifoliaes

The rootes of most kinds of these are about two or three inches long, (though some are flattish) roundish and knobby, or uneven, with severall knotts, with holes like to small eyes, from whence the stalkes come. They are of a darke browne color, and show like pieces of rotten stickes. The Leaves are shapt somwhat like to Colombine leaves, but they are stronger, harder, more hairy, and crumpled about the edges. On the top of each stalke stands one leafe, and it hath no more elsewhere, and this leafe shews like three, it is soe deeply cut into three parts. The stalke also that beareth a flower hath such a leafe growing about the middle of it.

The Flowers are either single, consisting commonly of seaven or eight long narrow leaves about a dove colour thrum, or dowble, with very many leaves, some more, some lesse.

The *Single* are usually of but one color'd leaves and a white bottome. The colours are Scarletts, Crimsons, Gridelines, Carnations, Pinkes, Whites and Ash colour. The striped are either Gridelines with white, or Scarletts.

These single kinds beare abundance of Flowers, and yield good

seed in March or Aprill. It is small and encompast ever with downe, from which it cannot easily bee seperated.
The D*owble* kinds wee call STAR Anemones, having many narrow thicke leaves in severall heights or degrees, lying spread open like a star or Marigold, shewing no thrum or seed in the middle of them. Commonly the backes of the lowest ranke of leaves of these starrs are all, or a great part, greene, and the rest of the flowers Gridelines, Redds, and Ash colours. And some are very beautifully stript, as the PAVO Maior, with a rich Scarlett and pure White, a very large lovely flower, but not very thicke; SUPERITS, Lemmon and White; BELLE d'ARRAS, tawney and white, and others.

All the Dowble as well as the single sorts above mentioned flower in MARCH or APRILL.

Many fine colour'd starrs have beene rais'd from the seed of the single Hard leav'd kinds, by a gentleman, one Mr Downton of Thistleworth neere London, but the PAVO Maior and the other stript ones come from beyond sea.
I know not any Flower soe nice and hard to bee humour'd in its culture as these starr Anemones. The single will blow well in any good mold and indifferent ayre, but the Dowble ones or starrs, though the rootes will live well enough abroad all wynter, yet the flowers will bee large and wellcolour'd but in few places, like the dowble yellow rose. The best way to treat them is to bestow on them very good rich mold, somwhat moist with old consum'd dung, to let them bee a very short tyme out of the ground, to water them often, and let them stand warme, but not too much expos'd to the sun.
When you remove them let it bee in the end of May or June, and plant them as soone againe as you can, but the seldomer remov'd the better.
Sow the seed of the dowble flowers or starrs, if you can get it, if not, of the single sorts, in potts or tubbs in August, in very

fine sifted earth, very thin, and cover it as lightly as may bee, and let them stand in the shade till wynter, unles you give them the morning sun somtymes. Water them somtimes, and then let them stand under a south wall, and bee well cover'd in frosts. When three yong leaves appeare, sift a little more fine mold on them, about the thicknes of the blade of a knife over them. When the leaves are wither'd sett them in the house, if you please. I have knowne this seed sowne in July in good mold under the shadow of fruite trees, presently after it is ripe, and only water'd sometimes with a small waterpot, doe very well. The seed is ripe in May, and must bee taken and gather'd as it rises up in the downe, in a sunny morning.

The French call these Hard Leav'd Anemones ANEMONES LIERRÉES or ANEMONES À DUR FEUILLAGE.

Of Soft or Thin Leav'd Anemones, or Tenuifoliaes

The rootes of these are not of soe darke a colour as the former, nor soe compacted into wood; few of them are long and round, but broadish flatt, with many little appendixes or Tongues, as Florists call them in England, as the Latine writers doe Lingulas, but the French PATTES, that is little pawes. The greene leaves are somwhat like parsley, only smaller and harder, and grow in three divisions of branches on the tops of the stalkes.

These have also, as the former, either Single or Dowble Flowers, both exceeding beautifull and tractable plants, not soe stubborne to bee cultivated as the Hard Leav'd kinds.

The *Single* are compos'd of six leaves, broader and every way larger than the Latifoliaes, standing about a purple thrum of seeds. They beare Flowers abundantly of almost all colors, as severall Gridelines, Crimsons, Scarletts, Carnations, Straw colours, Creame colours, Dove Colors and Whites. And some of these are stript, some bordered, others otherwise markt with white and other colours.

Their principall tyme of Flow'ring is MARCH & APRILL, but they will also, if not taken up in Sommer, beare all the Autumne and beginning of wynter.

They will prosper exceedingly in a fresh sifted mold from woodstacks, or gotten in the unploughed fields, mixt with store of old sifted dung of any kind, and need not bee sett in potts or hous'd in wynter, being hardy enough. But 'tis best raising the beds a little that the water may shed off, and let them stand in an open warme ayre, and to cover them with straw or mosse in the great frosts.

The Rootes are usually planted three or fower inches deepe in August or September, and taken up againe yearly in the end of May or June, and are to bee kept in a dry house till their replanting, as is before directed for Tulipes.

They may also bee kept out of the ground till the middle or end of February, and, then planted, will beare a while after the others sett in Autumne or sooner.

These single kinds yield excellent seeds with us (if they like the earth and aire) in the beginning of May, or soone after, which must bee gathered and sowne as is formerly directed for the seed of the Hard Leav'd Anemones, and from the seed of these single soft leav'd (the dowble soft leav'd yielding no seed) arise all the rare Dowble Plush Anemones, as wee call them, and the Hermaphrodites also.

The *Dowble* or soft leav'd kinds wee commonly call PLUSH Anemones, because they have often in the middle of their six broad leaves a great tuft like silke or PLUSH, but somtimes instead thereof some sorts have a great number of very small leaves, and others both small leaves and the silky tuft, by degrees above each other. Some sorts have the PLUSH, or little leaves, and the greater leaves wholy of one colour, as ye old CRIMSON, which was the first double soft leav'd Anemone wee had, the SCARLETT, the CARNATION, the PEACH, the GRIDELINE, the DOVE COLOUR, the FLESH COLOUR, the Pale LEMMON COLOUR, called in

French TRIPOLAINE, the DEEPE BROWNE or sad MURREY, called RANUNCULEE in French, all of small leaves, like the double Giant Rannunculus without any plush at all, the AMARANTHE, of a Murrey colour also with weake stalkes, the MORINE, of a deepe Violet color, the MARGUERITE of MARTILLETTI, all flame color, and two or three sorts of WHITE and some others.

PLUSH ANEMONES of severall colours in a flower are very much esteemed both here and abroad, and there is good variety of them, and great lovelines in them. Some are soe beautifull that they give place to noe flower whatsoever. Wee have rais'd none of these PLUSH Anemones here in England, but they come all originally from Italy and France. Monsieur Moryn, in his printed Catalogue, describes diverse sorts of them growing in his garden at Paris, which, because wee have most of them now growing in England, and not any other comparable to them, I have translated and inserted here:

ALBANOISE, all white except a little carnation in the bottome of the leaves and plush.
ALBERTINE or PASSESCALA, flesh color clouded with carnation.
ALBICANTE or CARNEE, the great leaves ill white, the plush white tipt with carnation.
ANGELICA, white leaves and pale grideline plush.
ASIATICKE, white and Carnation leaves, and scarlett and white plush.
ASTREA, white and carnation.
AUGUSTINE, white and carnation leaves and scarlett plush.
BOULONOISE, white leaves with carnation bottomes, the plush mixt with white, carnation and lemmon.
BRIOTE, white leaves mixt with carnation, the plush all carnation.
BUGI, all ill white and carnation mixt, the plush is white and small.
CANDIOTE, the leaves white grey with carnation bottomes, the plush carnation border'd with a greenish haire color.

CAZERTANE, the leaves crimson border'd with brimstone colour, the plush deepe scarlett.

CELESTINE, the leaves white, the plush soe too, but tipt with lemmon, which grows very pale with standing blowne.

CELIDEE, the leaves white and carnation, the plush rose color.

CLITIE, flesh colour and carnation.

DAMASINE, carnation and white, perfectly distinguisht.

DORISMENE, the leaves carnation and white, the plush reddish.

EXTRAVAGANTE, the leaves white, red, and greene, the plush of a strange form.

GABRIELE, white leaves, plush greene, white and carnation.

GALIPOLI of Thoulouze, all scarlett and white.

GAYETAN, the first flowers are white and purple, the last dove colour'd and peach.

HERISSEE, crimson leaves, somtimes stript with white, and scarlett plush.

JOLIVET, leaves flesh colour and crimson, the plush bricke color.

JULIANE, leaves white and carnation, plush carnation.

LIMOSINE, very like to the Extravagante.

LIONOISE, leaves and ruffe whitish grey with dove colour bottomes, plush dove colour tipt with greene.

MANTUANE, lemmon color with carnation bottomes.

MELIDORE, deepe scarlett, with white bottomes.

METELINE, all of a durty grey mixt with greene and carnation.

MORESQUE, all grey mixt with carnation.

MORETTE, leaves flesh color, plush white tipt with red.

NATOLIE, white and carnation all over.

NOIRON, crimson leaves, crimson and almost blacke plush.

ORIENTALLE, of a blew grey, like a slate's color.

PARISIENNE, white leaves, lemmon plush which grows white in tyme.

PARMESANNE, white leaves with red bottomes, the plush rose color, carnation and light haire colour.

PICARDE or JUNO, all white and peach.

PROVENSALLE, all greene and peach throughout.

QUATRICOLOR or AMARANTHE REGATE of fower sorts. The first crimson leaves stript with white, the plush Amaranthe colour, or a kind of Murrey with a red tuft in the midst; the second sort crimson leaves with Amaranthe plush, and a scarlett tuft border'd with white; the third sort called BELLE FRANCOISE, with white leaves mixt with some crimson, the plush murrey and the tuft carnation; the Fourth sort hath crimson leaves stript with white, the plush murrey, the tuft carnation.

REGATE, leaves and plush crimson and white, the flowers are great and the plush very large. An early flower.

ST CHARLES, ill white, & red towards the bottome.

SCALA, the leaves ill white, the plush scarlett.

SERMONETTA, all scarlett and pale yellow.

SYRIENNE, leaves pale Isabella clowded with flesh, plush light greene clowded with flesh.

TOSCANE, of a faded red, mixt with some haire color somtimes.

TURQUOISE, leaves and plush white, with carnation bottomes, the stalkes are long and stiffe, it flowers late.

VICTORIEUSE, flesh colour leaves mixt with carnation, plush haire colour and carnation.

There will dayly arise many new sorts of those Plush Anemones, soe many begin to sow the seed of the single Tenuifoliaes out of which they come, for the plush sorts seede not, but the sharpe springs and wett wynters, as well as frosts in England, will ever hinder us from having the finest sorts in that largnes and perfection of colors and markings as they have in the hotter countreys. Paris hath some very good, but Rome exceeds all places for this sort of Anemones.

There are great disputes amongst Florists about the best tyme to plant the plush kinds in England, and whether in potts or in full earth abroad. In my experience I find the best sorts generally very tender, and will not prosper out of potts, but some of the

rest will doe very well sett in a border of fine rich mold, under an east or south wall, being cover'd with mosse or something else in frosts, and the worst sorts in any of yr beds.
The larger the vessels are you plant them in the better, in the bottomes of which put good store of dung, but let it not touch the rootes, and make the earth you lay them in and that you cover them with two or three inches thicke very fine and sifted, compounded of fine earth and rotted dung, and a little willow earth, if you can get it.
As for the tymes of planting, I conceave August and February the best, though any tyme of the Autumne, or Spring either may serve, if they bee well water'd.
In the beginning of June, or at furthest by the middle of July, in dry weather take up all your good sorts, and lay them up in the house to dry, with some earth sticking to them, not too thicke together for heating and moulding, and before you plant them againe free them from the earth, and devide such great rootes as will easily part, and pare off the rottennes. The weaker or sicke rootes must bee sett in a more sandy earth than the other.
The Chiefe tyme of their flowring is March and Aprill.

Of Hermafrodite Anemones

These are New Sorts, not knowne till of late, comming from seed of the new Tenuifoliaes, having flowers somwhat like the starrs, and leaves like the tenuifolia's. The flowers have no greene markes on the backsides of their leaves as the starrs have, many of them. I have not seene any of them stript as yet, but of these colors: Scarlet, Crimson, Flesh colour, Pale Grideline, Deepe Grideline, Greys or Ashcolours.
These are as tender and delicate as any of the Plush kinds, and must bee us'd like them. They flower at the same tyme with them. We esteeme them yet very much.

OF TUBEROUS IRISES, or Flower de lys

There are two kinds. The GREAT FLAGD *leav'd, and the* SMALLER, *of which last there are also two sorts, one growing high, and the other* DWARFES, *called* CHAMAIRIDES.

Of Great Flagged Irises *wee have* severall colours, as DEEPE BLEW, PALE BLEW, ASH COLOUR, WHITE, PURPLE, Flesh Colour, and some few with two or more colours, one of which hath blew standards and peach falls.

Of the other Flaggs, that are not Dwarfes, there are the White, the Yellow, the light Blew, the Deeper Blew, the Purple, the Chalcedonian or blacke Grey, the pure white, edged and stript downe the backe with light watchet, the Purple vein'd with Yellow, and many other varietyes, too long to bee here mention'd. These and the great Flaggs take up soe much roome in a garden with their leaves that the bulbous Irises are preferred before them, yet they doe well in large grounds. Their flowers are thin leav'd and therfore are quickly spoil'd with wett or great heates.

Both the abovementioned Flaggs flower in Aprill and May.

The Dwarfes are of many single colours, as Blews, Greys, Ash-colours, Purples, Greenes, and wee have diverse of two or more colors.

These flower very early in the Spring.

All the Flaggs except the Chalcedonian are hardy, and grow well in any good mold, enduring all cold weather, and neede not bee taken up yearly. Shade is more agreable to them than hot sun, but they ought not to bee dropt upon from the boughes of trees. They multiply exceedingly from the rootes, and will grow being planted at any tyme, if water'd. The seed comes to perfection with us, and will produce new kinds being sowne, but wee neglect these sorts of Irises in respect of the Bulbous.

Most of the rootes are great and round like a Turnep, but of a darke browne colour. The leaves are shapt like Ivy leaves generally, but some sorts have them rounder at the point. They are finely wrought with a darke greene color, and a light color whitish, and in the middle figured into hearts, whereof some are of the darke color, and are called blacke hearts, and some are of the light, and called white hearts.

The flowers are only one on every stalke, standing at the top thereof, the long small leaves of them turne back, shewing an open round mouth or cup, commonly ring'd about with purple.

The stalkes are red, and the seed is small & round.

Wee have now Fower sorts of Cyclamens, differenced by their season of flowering, as

The SPRING kinds, which are of two sorts; one with a very sweete White flower, and another with a Flesh color, lesse sweete.

They begin to Flower in MARCH and continue till MAY.

The SOMMER kinds are The Cyclamen of VERONA, which hath a round leafe and purple flowers, and that of MOUNT LIBANUS, with very large pale Flesh coloured flowers, the roote hereof hath fibers only under the bottome of the roote, and not as the rest upon it.

These flower in JULY, AUGUST & SEPTEMBER.

The AUTUMNE kinds are the Roman and the Ivy leaf'd, both which beare white & purple flowers, but not sweete, in AUGUST & SEPTEMBER.

The WYNTER Cyclamens are the commoner sort which hath small purplish flowers, and that of PERSIA, rare with us.

These blow the most part of the Wynter.

The CYCLAMEN of ANTIOCH is sayd to bee of both the aforementioned colours, and to blow in the Spring and Autumne, & to come somtimes dowble, but I have not seene it in England.

The Spring kinds are not soe hardy as the Autumnall, they must stand under a warme South or East wall, and bee cover'd in the hard weather, whereas the other need not such care. The nature of the wynter kind is not yet well understood by us. The Cyclamens of Verona and Mount Libanus are in few hands in England, and are kept in potts, being tenderer than the Spring sorts.

All the sorts require a fine rich mold, and must bee seldome remov'd, but the tyme of their transplanting is presently after their greene leaves are wither'd away, which spring not out of the ground untill the flowers are almost past, except it bee that of Mount Libanus, which hath both leaves & flowers together. They are encreased by cutting the great round rootes to pieces, every piece whereof will grow, if it hath one of the little holes in it, which are in severall places of the roote.

But the best way of multiplying them is by the seed, if you can have patience three yeares. That of the Spring kinds is to bee sowne in the Spring, as that of the Autumnall kinds in the Autumne. Sow them in fine rich sifted dung and mold, in potts or cases, and water them often, give them sun somtimes, and cover them in frosts. The seed becomes first a little Tuber, and then puts forth leaves.

The pieces of the rootes you cut to plant must bee kept out of the ground three or fower days, to dry the hurt a little, and then the wound must bee cover'd with soft red wax and a little turpentine, and soe put into the earth very shallow, and not water'd upon their setting.

OF THE TUBEROUS HYACINTH

This only Tuberous Hyacinth wee have is much differing from the other bulbous hyacinths, for the flowers of this sort are much larger

than any of the rest, and shapt like a Lilly. The leaves are of a yellowish greene color, weake and long, not soe fatt and thicke as those of the Bulbous Hyacinths. The rootes are long and whitish, and encrease much with offsetts.
They come forth of the ground in the beginning of Spring.
The flowers are pure white, and as sweet as Orenge or Jasmyn flowers.

It flowers from the end of JUNE to the end of AUGUST. Wee have had this plant in England but lately, and find the rootes very subject to rott and dye with frosts and rains, though by reason of the great encreases thereof by offsetts wee preserve some still alive.
It is best planted in very rich fine dry sifted mold in a pott, which must bee thrust into a hott bed up to the top in February to make the roote strike out fibers quickly, for after that it will live well enough. Cover the pott with mosse while it is in the bed, and water it not at all there. When there are yong leaves cover it also in the night and sharpe weather, and then the leaves having some strength, remove the pott into a border of earth under a south wall, being there thrust up to the brim into the ground, cover it there nightly constantly with a glasse and a little mosse under it, and in the cold parts of the day also, till it begin to put forth buds to flower, and then you may take up the pot and give it ayre, and water plentifully. Take up the rootes in September, or when the leaves are wither'd, and keepe them forth of the earth till February.

THE HOLLOW ROOT

I adde this here because the roote is soe like the Cyclamens, but 'tis yellow within, and very hollow underneath. The leaves are somewhat like to Colombines, and are only above ground in the Spring. It hath a long spike of flowers shapt somwhat like as the Larkesheeles, with spurrs, but with a little greene leafe at the foot of each flower.

Wee have TWO SORTS, one with ill faint red or purple flowers, another with white flowers which is the stronger and better kind.
It flowers in the Spring.
It growes without trouble in good garden mold, if the place bee sheltered from the cold, and is encreased by pieces of the rootes. The seed is round and blackish.

OF SATYRIUMS, or Orchides Palmatae

These differ most from the other Orchises in their Tuberous rootes, for the flowers and leaves are not much unlike. They are called Palmatae, because the rootes are shapt like to a hand, with fingers at the bottomes of the stalkes, they put out small fibers from the bottomes which bear spikes of little flowers.

The kinds wee have are these

SATYRIUM BASILICUM MAS, the Male Royall Satyrium, called also the Male Palma Christi, which hath a spike of flesh colour'd flowers markt with a deeper red. The great leaves are long and greene, and there is a small leafe at the foot of the stalke of each flower.
SATYRIUM BASILICUM FEMINA, the Female Satyrium, or the Female Palma Christi, which hath commonly white flowers markt with purple but is sometimes of the same colours as the former. The greene leaves are longer, narrower, and more spotted than the former. They flower in June and July, and delight in moist Meadow Earth, where they grow naturally with us.

OF DRAGONS, or the Great SERPENTARIA

Dragons have great round and high stalkes, much spotted with red spotts, and with some very deepe cutt or jagged greene leaves on the tops of them, amongst which, on another long stalke, comes a long smooth tawney pestle out of a hose, greene on the outside and shining purple within. Unles the roote bee old this pestle appeares not, which is all the beauty of the plant, for it hath no flower besides.

This pestle comes forth in JUNE.
Dragons require a rich garden mold, and to stand unremov'd under some warme wall, and are encreast from the roote, which is white.

The ARUMS may bee referred to this place having much resemblance to this Serpentaria.

OF GLANDULOUS FLOWERS

This sort of flowers is commonly ranked by writers under the Tuberous, but there is a great difference and dissimilitude betwixt them in their rootes in my opinion, and therefore I have made another classe of them. Wee tearme them Glandulous from the Latine word Glandule, which signifies a fleshy lump or kernell of a man's body. The PEONY, *the* ASPHODILL *and the* PHALANGIUM ALLOBROGICUM *have greater glandules or bunches hanging together for their rootes than the* RANUNCULES, *or* CERANIUM TRISTE *or* DOWBLE PALEWORT *have, which are all the kinds of Glandulous flowers considerable to bee treated of.*

OF THE PEONY

There are severall SINGLE *and* DOWBLE *flower'd* PEONYES.

The SINGLE are the RED or CRIMSON MALE, the RED FEMALE, the FLESH colour'd FEMALE, the White FEMALE, and the Deepe RED of CONSTANTINOPLE, which hath large flowers consisting of eight leaves, the other single kinds not having above five or six, and the Deepe Murrey or BLACKE, as it is called, this is very rare.

Of DOWBLE Peonyes *wee have* the COMMON CRIMSON, the BLUSH Colour (this turnes not white), the DEEPER CRIMSON, or the PURPLE, as it is usually called, whose greene leafe is smaller & lighter & not soe deepe cutt as the former, the CARNATION, or light pinke colour, which is yet somwhat rare. The flower of this kind withers on the stalke, and shedds not its leaves as the other sorts doe.

They all flower in MAY.
And all prosper well abroad all the yeare in our gardens, and may bee remov'd at any tyme, but best in Autumne, and are easily encreast from their rootes and seed.

OF ASPHODILLS

Wee have only these with Glandulous rootes:

The YELLOW, in Roote and Flowers, this is that wee call in English the Kingspeare, in Latine Hastula Regia. It beares in Aprill, and hath a spike of small flowers which lye open like starrs.
The WHITE UNBRANCHT, with a spike of white flowers, starr fashion, of five leaves apiece, with some darke purple streakes on the backsides. The seed is like Buck or French Wheat.
The WHITE BRANCHT, having larger white flowers than the former, and therfore more valued. These last TWO sorts flower in MAY & JUNE.

These grow without trouble in ye gardens, and are best remov'd in September and October.

OF LILLY ASPHODILLS

These are betwixt Lillyes and Asphodills, the flowers being large and not many on a stalke. We have only the ORENGE, which is called the Day Lilly, continuing in flower but a day, and the YELLOW. These blow in May, before the other Lillyes, and the Orenge first.

OF PHALANGIUM ALLOBROGICUM, or Savoy Spiderwort

This hath fower or five long narrow greene leaves, a round stiffe stalke of about a foot high, with seaven or eight flowers of a pure white color, with chives tipt with yellow, and like in shape and greatness to the Day Lilly.
It flowers in Aprill and May.
It is a tender plant and beautifull, and not common in England, it must bee ordered as other tender flowers that stand abroad all wynter, and kept little out of the earth.

OF GERANIUM TRISTE, the Sweete Cranesbill

This plant is very scarce in England, and of great sweetnes in the night time. The roote is glandulous or buncht, the stalke is round, rough, tender, and joynted about a hand high. The leaves are large and jagged of a darke greene, they lye on the ground presently. The stalkes beare on their tops umbells of flowers in shape like the other cranesbills, of a faint yellow color, spotted with two purple spotts on each leafe of the flower. After the flowers follow long, sharpe, pointed bills, with red long seed in the bottomes thereof. It is often called Geranium noctu olens, because of its excellent sweet smell in the night only, and Geranium Triste, because it rejoyceth not in the day.

It flowers in June, and most part of the Sommer.

It will not live the wynter with us if not potted and hous'd, or otherwise cover'd abroad under some warme wall. It requires very good fine mold, and ought not to bee kept long out of the earth. It is encreast easily from the rootes and seed.

A pott of it in flower will perfume a room sufficiently in the night time.

OF RANUNCULES

The Glandulous kind of Ranunculus (for there are others) have their rootes consisting of very small knobs, like graines of wheate, and are usually called in Latine Ranunculi Asiatici, Ranunculus of Asia, and in French Ranuncules de Tripoly, of Tripoly, a towne in Barbary. The stalkes are many, long and hairy as the leaves also are, which are fatt and thicke, and devided commonly into three divisions, of a yellowish greene colour. There are SINGLE *and* DOWBLE *sorts, both beautifull.*

Of the SINGLE *wee have* the WHITE, the DEEPE YELLOW, the PALE YELLOW, the MURREY or DEEPE RED, the GOLD YELLOW stript through with Scarlet, that called AURORA, of a deepe yellow colour markt on the outside with scarlet, the ROSE frizè, WHITE with rose color on the backe, the PASSE ROSE with the inside white, and the outside damaske rose colour clouded with white, the ROMAN, chamois colour within, and soe on the backe but markt with red, the AFRICAN, yellow within, and yellow and scarlett without, the BESANSON, yellow within and pale yellow and red without, the CLOTH of GOLD, of that color, the MELIDOR, all pale Isabella within, and crimson edg'd with the same Isabella without, the PARMESAN, yellow within, and gold color border'd with crimson without, SATINNE, white within, and white marked with red without, the SYDONIAN, Chamois within, and chamois markt with red without.

Most of the single kinds that have names were soe called at first in Paris in France, from whence they came but lately to us. They have all a blacke wrought head or button in the midst of each flower, wherein is contain'd long, flat, small reddish seed.

Of DOWBLE Ranunculus *wee have* the Giant of Rome, of an Orenge color.

The Giant of Constantinople, of a deeper Orenge Red, and a larger thicker flower.

The Greater Orenge, stript with yellow.

The Lesser Orenge, stript with a better, more distinct yellow than the former; neither of these grow neere soe high as the two firsts, nor have soe large flowers.

The Yellow, which came out of the little Orenge, and is very scarce yet.

They all flower in Aprill and May.

The best time to plant them is about Christmas in potts, or in full rich earth. If in potts they must bee often water'd and set sometimes in the sun. If abroad, cover them in frosts in wynter and spring with mosse.

Take up the rootes yearly in June or July, and keepe them dry in the house till December, when you are to plant them.

Sow the seed as other fine seeds in very small sifted mold in potts or cases in the beginning of Spring, or as soone as it is ripe, and order it afterwards as Tulipe or Anemone seed sowne. It will produce often new sorts.

There is another sort with a leafe like Rew, and a golden yellow small dowble flower, which is in flower in Aprill, & may bee planted in October, for it endures the frosts.

Pilewort is the same as Celandine, in Latine Cheledonium.

This wee mention here is the lesser Pilewort, for there is a greater Pilwort with fibrous rootes. The leaves are round, smooth and shining like the Ivy. The Flowers are dowble and of a yellow color, & are soone shedd with wett.

This plant is of no great beauty or consideration, and grows easily in any good earth, in any garden.

It flowereth in MARCH, and the leaves come up a little before the flowers, and are wither'd away before May.

OF FIBROUS FLOWERS

Wee are now come to the Fowerth and last sort of flowers, which are such as have FIBROUS *or* STRINGY *Rootes of which (as hath beene already sayd) there are* TWO KINDS; *one whose rootes continue many yeares and are therefore called* PERENNIALLS, *after the Latine word Perennis, the other whose rootes dye yearly, and are therefore also after the Latine usually called* ANNUALLS, *and these are only perpetuated by their seed.*

OF PERENIALL FIBROUS FLOWERS

and First of GILLIFLOWERS, *called in Latine Cariophylli, and in French* OEILLETS.

Wee have very great varietyes of very fine ones, some all of one color, some of two, some stript with long great flakes, others most speckled or spotted only, and many having names.

Gilliflowers consisting most of *Scarlet* color in esteeme at present are the Morillion triumphant, the Incarnadine de Bland, the Imperiall of Holland, the Jewell (very good deepe scarlett, faire flower, breaks not) The Nonpareille, the Pucelle, the Catuse, the Adonis, the Thisbe, the French Merveille, the Piccolomini, the Belle Astrea, the Belle Eudique, the Dorothy, Belle Belin (good middle sized flower, breaks not) the Generall Dortoon, the Cesarini, the Belle Princesse, the Bride of Holland, the Cher Amy, the Grave Mansfelt, & Bezar's Tawney.

Of Pinkes and Pale Reds wee have Augustus, the Admirall of Zealand, la Croix, Faire Francis.

Of lighter Crimsons the Virgin of Collen, Prince of Condè, Lusthof, Master de Camp, St Lambert, Rosamund, Seraphicke, Cupidon Royall, Parismus, Lady of the Abbey, Rosella, Galathea, Beminda, Hertoch Leopold, Grand Turban, Venetian, Genrall Coman, Alexander the Great, Rosiliante.

Of Deeper Crimsons Breze Tout, Great Dan, Blacke Imperiall,

Pollinates, Morillion Nonpareille, Browne Appelles, Lamasoon, Dunkerwolke.

Of Murreys we have the Grey Hulo, Wiggens, Amelia, New blacke, Imperiall, Grave Floras.

Of Gridelines and Purples Philomell or the Nightingale, Nimph Royall, Bethlem, Prince of Wales, Belle Angloise, Turloone, Spetieuse, Belle Borsure, Jasper, Tapisseere, Insulare, Princess Royall, very good flower, breaks not.

The *Newest* of severall colors are these, Queen Hesther, crimson & white, large flower, The Wonder of the World, a very large flower, but breakes much, light crimson and white, Sigismond, Van Koell, Alexander of Holland, the King of Portugall, reasonable large flower, a kind of deepe murrey & white.

They begin to flower in the end of June, are in their chiefe glory in July, and thence called July flowers, and goe out in the end of August, though somtymes some continue longer, as some wynter podds blow as early as May.

Gilliflowers agree best to bee rais'd in a very loose blacke mold mixt with some old sifted dung, and a little sand.
Such an earth makes the flowers fairer and more in number than too fatt a soyle which makes them run into leaves and branches too much.
They are best preserv'd in good large earthern potts, that they may bee remov'd up and downe as the weather is, and the season of the yeare. There is no flower more subiect to dye, either with the frosts of wynter, the wynds of Spring, the violent drought and heate of sommer, or much raines at any tyme of yeare, therefore they need an experienced and careful gardiner to looke to them and one must bee stored with great numbers of them to have a sufficient quantity in Sommer, for many will dye every yeare, let the care of them bee never soe great.

They must bee hous'd in the extremity of wynter, but not choked up for want of ayre. They must bee set abroad in the daytime in the fayre weather in February, and hous'd againe in the nights. They must not stand abroad constantly till the end of March, unles they bee very well shelter'd with hedges or walls from wynd. In Aprill and May they must bee throughly water'd at a tyme, but not too often, for many are rotted or lost with too much watering. In March put fine fresh sifted mold to the rootes pretty high neere the leaves, which will very much refresh them, and keepe away the cold wynds, which kill more in this moneth than the wynter frosts, the hott sun also of March is very destructive to them. In the end of March cut off the wither'd leaves and stalkes, and put red wax on the tops of the stalkes, that the cold pierce them not.

As soone as they begin to podd for flowers you must sticke up two or three long stickes in every pott, and tye the branches gently up to them, and hang sheepes hoofes on the tops of the stickes or hollow canes to take the Earewiggs which will creepe thereinto for shelter in the daytyme, and may there bee found dayly, and destroyed, otherwise they will eat up the yong podds and soe spoil the flowers.

About Midsomer begin to lay downe all the lower branches on every roote which are not like to beare, cutting a ioynt in the wood halfe through, and pinning them downe into the earth with a little wooden hooke or other sticke, and covering the sticke and the branch with earth, letting the tops of the sprigges stand above ground with the leaves, which tis best to clip even on the tops with your sisers, as you doe slips when you set them. You may continue laying branches still as they grow out long enough for the purpose almost all the sommer, and there are little laying potts with slitts on one side to set upon stickes to draw in thereunto such branches as grow high. Those little potts are filled with good fine earth.

In three weekes or a moneth's tyme commonly these layers will bee rooted, or not at all, and then they must be remov'd into other good mold, cutting the stalke off from the mother roote, and being careful not to hurt the yong fibers. Being planted they must bee water'd gently, and set in the shade till they grow strongly, and then may bee remov'd whither you please. These layers will better endure the next wynter than the old rootes, and some rootes will afford half a score or more of such layers. Take off some of the smallest pods of yr best gilliflowers, that the rootes spend not themselves in bearing too many flowers, and if your pods break, tye them about with thread or leather, or such things.

If you perceave the tops of the greene leaves to grow white or frett, cut off all as far as it is infected, covering the tops of the stalkes with a little soft wax, melted with turpentine. Many dye thus downward, and commonly with drought, therfore water them well at such tymes, and prune them as aforesaid.

Keepe the seeds of the fairest largest pods of all colors, espetially Orenges and whites, and gather it in a fayre day, when it is full ripe.

Sow the seed as soon as it is gather'd, in fine sifted mold, set it in the shade, and water it with a small pot. When the leaves are an inch high give them a little sun, and as they are bigg enough to transplant take them up, letting the smaller rootes stand. They will beare the next yeare, if sowne as soon as the seed is ripe, but it may bee sowne also in Autumne or the Spring, but then the yong rootes will not beare that yeare.

Most of ye best Gilliflowers come out of Flanders yearly, and some out of Holland; wee raise but few great flowers here, though some use all the art possible to doe it.

OF STOCKE GILLIFLOWERS

In Latine they are called Leucoia Incana, and in French Girofles. Wee have diverse colors of the single sort, as a deepe violet, a bright light crimson, a pure white and a creame color, which is the sweetest, and some dowble, of purples or tawny colours, which are many tymes finely stript or markt with white. They write of a dowble yellow, but 'tis a stranger yet in England.

Old rootes will beare flowers in MARCH, APRILL, & MAY espetially, but the seedlings most moneths of sommer, as they were sowne early or late.

They must have a very good loose warme mold, and must bee hous'd in wynter, I meane the dowble sorts (for the other are not worth the paines). All the care that can bee us'd is little enough to preserve them in long Frosts.

They may bee encreast from cuttings set in moist earth in a shady place, but best from the seed of the single kinds, the dowble afford none. Wee cannot certainly find out what seed beares most dowble flowers, sometimes there will bee many rootes of a little seed, and sometimes not one dowble flower of much seed.

The seed is flat and yellowish, the single kinds will sometimes live abroad two or three wynters.

OF WALLFLOWERS

These are the third sort of flowers which are called in Latine LEUCOIA, *they are also called* KEIRI, *and by us Wallflowers, because the single ones grow usually upon old castle or stone walls.*

The single sorts are only of two colours, YELLOW and WHITE, which is yet rare, as the first is most common.

Of the dowble *wee have* the YELLOW also, very sweet, and the GREAT YELLOW, markt with blood red spotts or flakes. There is also a DOWBLE WHITE, but 'tis very scarce and tender.

All flower from FEBRUARY to MAY, but they flourish most in MARCH.

They are, all but the White, easily preserv'd in a warme place abroad all wynter in good garden mold, but the White must bee potted and hous'd.

They are usually encreast from slipps, and from the seed of the single ones.

OF BEARES EARES, or AURICULAS

AURICULA URSI *in Latine, this flower is a kind of Cowslip, agreeing much with it in the sent and figure of the flowers, but different much in the greene leaves. It is very sweet, very various, very hardy, easily encreast, and soone at perfection, of a fine forme, and beautifull colours, and agrees admirably well with ye Climate, soe that it may seeme for all these good qualityes not inferiour to any flower this Countrey can produce.*

The sorts of this Flower are not to bee numb'red, nor the colours of all of them to bee fittly named or described. Wee have White, Yellowes of all sorts, Haire colours, Orenges, Cherry colours, Crimson and other Redds, Violetts, PURPLES, MURREYS, TAWNEYS, OLIVES, CINNAMON Colours, ASH color, DUNNS, and what not? but wee esteeme most such as have great and white eyes in the middle of the flowers, and most flowers on a stalke, if it bee strong and high.

Faire Yellow Eyes are also good, and generally such Eyes as endure raine best, and are longest in washing away. There are some sorts border'd or stript with two colours besides the Eye, but only two such esteem'd, the one stript with White, which is a kind of Tawney or Purple, reasonable common, the other Purple and Yellow colour, very rare.

Diverse of the Hairecolours, or LEATHER COATES, as they are usually tearm'd, have had names impos'd upon them, as TUGGEYS, LANCYES, LOOKERS, HUMFREYS and other Leathercoates, and some PURPLES, as the EMPEROUR, the PRINCE of WALES, BELLE BRUNETTE, &c, some ORENGES as the PRINCE of ORENGE, the ROYALL ORENGE, and some others as the DOWNHAM, of a good violet colour.

The CHIEFE SEASON of their Flowering is MARCH and beginning of APRILL, but they beare a little againe in August and September. They cannot have too rich a soyle, nor almost too moist if it bee rich. They prosper not out of the shade, and yet should stand warme there, as in a border under a wall. Many use to pott them, but they will doe as well abroad, if they bee a little cover'd in Frosts, and thrust into the earth after the thawes have borne them up out of the ground. If they bee set in potts they must bee well water'd.

In the end of February fresh mold should bee set to the top of the rootes, which will comfort them exceedingly, and defend them from the piercing March wynds.

The Leathercoates have generally a larger whiter mealy leafe than the PURPLES or Murreys have, but some few Reds have also mealy leaves.

The rootes encrease much, and some sorts divide easily into parts, which may bee soe parted and set at any tyme, but best about Michelmas (or in the end of August).

The seed is ripe in JUNE, and best sowed in OCTOBER, though it may doe well in February. The first sower of them was one TUGGEY in Westminster about thirty yeares since, who rais'd some good ones out of a great Leathercoate bearing his name, but now many sow and have found out the certain way, and raise new fine sorts every yeare.

The best way is this:

Take good blacke mold, mix it with rotten cow dung, fill pans or boxes with it within a foot or lesse of the brimms, then sift thereon a little sand mixt with salt to keepe worms away, then sift on that Willow earth above an inch thicke, otherwise soe much of the finest light old rotten dung, on which scatter your seed pretty thicke, and passe through a very fine sieve soe much of the same flower of dung or willow earth as will but just hide the seed from birds and keepe it from being blowne away by the wind. Let it stand soe abroad all wynter in some shady place, covering the vessells with matts or mosse in great frosts and snowes and violent raines, that the seed bee not uncover'd by them.

In the end of Aprill or beginning of May the seed will come up very thicke, if it hitt right, and after June you may bee still removing the forwardest rootes into other potts or places filled with fine mold, and out of the hott sun, where they may have room to grow, which may bee againe transplanted when you please.
Water them often upon each of their removings, and give them little sun, and the next yeare they will beare flowers, and the best commonly first.

OF HEPATICAES

The Hepatica hath a fine great tuft of dark greene trefoile leaves, before which a little come the flowers, each on a small stalke of its owne. There are only TWO *with Dowble Flowers, one of a rich Blew color, the other a red or flesh color. The Single are of severall colours, as* WHITE, PALE BLEW, DEEPE BLEW, *Light* BLUSH *and* DEEPE BLUSH *full of little threads.*
They all flower in February, and commonly the Dowble one first.
The greene leaves dye all at the approach of wynter, and spring forth againe with, or soone after, the flowers.
The plant loves a warme rich mold, and a station under or neere some wall or other place that shelters it from the winds, otherwise they are hardy enough and need not housing, but the Dowble kind never beares faire large flowers in smoaky townes, but delights in a pure ayre.
The English name is Liverwort, but 'tis commonly called Hepatica by all.
The roote is best remov'd or divided about Michelmas, being in flower soe early in the Spring.

OF LYCHNISES

There is more than one Speties of Plants called in Latine by this name, for wee have Lychnis Coronaria, which is ye CAMPION, *where-*

of some sorts have single Red and others single White Flowers, and one sort hath a Dowble Crimson Flower.

Then there is Lychnis Sylvestris, wh. wee call BATCHELOURS BUTTONS, with Dowble Red and White flowers.

The third sort differs much from any of the former, and is the most esteemed and new. Wee call it LYCHNIS CHALCEDONICA, or CONSTANTINOPOLITANA, the Lychnis of Constantinople or Chalcedon. And of this kind there is a single Scarlet or rather Orenge, and a White, which is the rarer, though lesse beautifull, and a Dowble Scarlet, or rich Crimson.
This Lychnis of Constantinople hath long rough hairy stalkes, and is therefore in Latine tearm'd Hirsuta, with severall ioynts, and two small leaves at every ioynt. The flowers grow many together on the top of the stalke, of fine narrow long leaves of the single kind, and three or fower heights of such leaves of the dowble sort (which beareth no seed as the single doth, which seed is blacke and small).
This Lychnis flowers in the sommer moneths. It is somewhat tender, and is best preserv'd in potts, but Campions and Batchelours Buttons grow all wynter abroad in most gardens.
All are usually encreast from their rootes, which are easily divided, and planted betimes in the SPRING in good rich mold.

OF TRACHELIUM AMERICANUM, or PLANTA CARDINALIS, the Cardinall's flower

It is called, I thinke, the Cardinall's Plant from the rich Scarlett flowers, some writers name it also RAPUNTIUM MAXIMUM *Coccineo spicato flore. The roote is very small, white and fibrous, the leaves are fatt, somwhat indented, of a sad greene color, apt to lye on the earth. The stalkes are round, hollow, two foote high at least, brancht upwards, with many flowers at the tops of a rich* SCARLET *colour, shapt like single Larkes Spurrs, with a little greene leafe at the foote of each flower stalke. The flower hath no sent, and produces a very small blacke round seed.*

It flourisheth from the beginning of JUNE most part of the sommer. It is tender, and must either stand under a south wall, or bee potted to bee hous'd in wynter, and the stalkes when they grow high must bee supported with long stickes, as gilliflowers are when they grow neere flowering.

Wee have not tryed the seed much whether it will bring varietyes, but encrease the plant by dividing the rootes, and planting them with good fine rich earth in the Spring.

LILLY of the VALLEY

In Latine Lilium Convallium, it hath a very stringy roote, which spreads farr neere the surface of the earth, and hath many knotts. The greene leaves are in colour and shape like those of the white Lillyes, but much lesse. The flowers are small, hanging many on a tough branch with open mouths, like grape hyacinthes in good order. They are very sweet.

Wee have of them TWO *Colours.*

A WHITE, which is common,

and a BLUSH colour, which is very scarce.

They flower in the end of APRILL and in MAY, and the leaves continue not all the yeare.

They grow without trouble abroad in ye gardens all wynter, and best in warme yet shadowed places. They are easily encreast from their rootes.

OF SPIDERWORTS

In Latine Phalangia. Besides the Savoy Spiderwort with a glandulous roote spoken of before, wee have TWO KINDS *with Fibrous or stringy rootes that are pereníalls.* The first sort hath long narrow grassy leaves, and a stalke above a cubit high, with many small starr flowers, consisting of six white leaves apiece, like starr hyacinthes, with pale yellow threads in the middle. Of this kind there are two diversityes, one brancht and the other not, there is also another lesser one, with a purple veine downe the midst of each leafe of the flower, which flowers in MAY, as the two first doe in JUNE. The second is a new sort, called the VIRGINIA SPIDERWORT, because it came first from thence into England. It resembles the other only in the greene leaves, but this hath larger ones than the former, and stronger and more ioynts of stalkes. The flower consists only of three leaves, pretty large and poynted, which being blowne lye flatt open in the day, and are drawne in the night into a huske of three little greene leaves which sustain the flower, and stand upon very weake foot-stalkes. In the midst of the flower are small chives tipt with yellow. On the tops of the stalkes are many of these flowers, which blow one after another for a long time.

That which was brought out of Virginia had a DEEPE fowle BLEW color, and from the seed thereof there have beene rais'd in England other colour'd flowers which are not yet common, they are these:

One with a WHITE flower.

Another with a BLUSH.

Another with a good REDDISH PURPLE.

And Another with a LIGHT BLEW, whose flower is lesser than the rest.

All have chives tipt with yellow in the middle.

These VIRGINIANS are in flower from JUNE to the end of SEPTEMBER.

They ought to stand in a good earth, and a warme place in a garden, and will soe live abroad well all wynters. They are easily encreast by dividing their rootes in October or thereabouts and by sowing their seed which often brings forth new kinds.

OF VALERIANS

There are two that are called GREEKE VALERIANS, *one with many small blew flowers of five leaves apiece, and small white chives tipt with yellow. Another with white flowers, like it in all things but the color.*

There are also Two VALERIANS bearing DODONEUS his name, one with abundance of small reddish flowers, like those of the Laurustine before they are full out, and another with white flowers.

These flower all MAY and JUNE, and are kept without trouble in ye gardens, and encreast from their rootes Spring and Autumne.

INDIAN CANES

Wee have two wee value

One with an ORIENT CRIMSON colour'd flower, like the Gladiolus of Constantinople.

Another with a Yellow flower, spotted with red spots.

They have both high stalkes which perish yearly to the rootes, and long flaggy pointed leaves. Both are very tender, and must stand under a warme wall in good earth, and the rootes must bee cover'd in frosts.

They flower in August, and are best encreast from their seed.

TUFTS, Thlaspi

The flowers are only very many small threads, standing umbellwise on the tops of the branches, like tufts of silke. Their greene leaves are like Colombines. The rootes are yellow long strings, the seed is long and small. The chiefe differences are the GREAT WHITE SPANISH, and that of CANADA with PURPLISH flowers described by Cornutus.

The first flowers in MAY, ye other in JUNE.

OF MARACOCS, or Passion flowers

The Maracoc is called in Latine GRANADILLA *and* CLEMATIS TRIFOLIA, *and* FLOS PASSIONIS, *the Passion flower, because there are some parts of the flower which resemble a speare and three nayles, the instruments of the passion.*

The flower consists of ten Whitish leaves, which stand round and are cover'd with many crooked threads of a kind of pale PEACH color, with a ring or circle of deepe peach. Out of the middle of the flower comes a pale whitish greene head spotted with red, with five crooked spotted hornes with broadish heads, from the midst of which rises another head, which beares three things like nayles, bigg above, and smaller below, greenish at the topps. The flowers are sweet. The plant is a climber and must bee supported. The leaves are fashion'd like figg leaves, which together with the stalkes dye yearly downe to the rootes, and spring forth againe in May.

There is another newer sort of Virginian Maracocs with a YELLOW flower.

Both flower in JULY and AUGUST.

They are tender, and must bee kept in potts to bee hous'd in wynter, as other Indians, but they are not soe tender as some. The encreases must bee taken from the rootes in March.

OF LUPINES

Wee have onely one which is PERENIALL, *that is lives all wynter, and is therefore called the* EVERLASTING LUPINE, *it came not long since first hither from Virginia.*

It is of a good blew colour, and is in flower in Aprill and May. It must stand under a warme wall, where it will bring good seede, which flyes sodainly away when ripe, but if gather'd and sowed in the Spring it produces good effects. It is encreast also from the rootes in Spring & Autumne.

OF NIGELL, or MELANTHIUM

I shall mention only three sorts, all which are rather BIENNIALLS *that is live but two yeares, rather than Perennialls.*

The Great SPANISH NIGELL or Fennell flower, with the single pale blew flowers.
The Great Dowble Pale BLEW, with a greene round head in the midst, it is called in Latine Nigella Damascena flore maiore pleno caeruleo.
The lesser dowble WHITE, called often in Latine Nigella Catherina. This sort hath no greene fennel leaves behind the flower as the rest have.
They flower in May, June & July.
The Spanish Nigell is the most esteam'd and is somwhat tender, the rest grow without care in ye gardens. They are only encreast by the seed.

MOATH MULLEIN

In Latine Blattaria, and Verbascum. The Perenniall kinds are only these: that with the blacke roote and WHITE flower; that with a durty reddish yellow or BUFFE color'd flower, with red threads in the middle, somwhat rare; the SWEET YELLOW; and the PURPLE. The SAND color, with very large flowers, very rare.
All the kinds have many long spikes of flowers on high stiffe stalkes, all along the stalkes, two or three foote high. The leaves are great and long, somwhat like the Foxgloves.
All which flower in May and June. They grow easily in good earth in our gardens, and are encreased from their rootes and seed.

CORTUSA MATHIOLI

Broad leav'd Mountaine SANICLE, *in English, and* SANICULA ALPINA *also in Latine. It hath torne ragged leaves which perish yearly. The flowers stand many on a stalke like Beares Eares, and are of a deepe purple colour, with white eyes.*
It flowers in the end of May and JUNE.
Wee use to keepe this flower in potts.

BELLS

In Latine Campanulae. There are severall flowers wee call Bells, but

here I meane those with the long narrow darke greene leafe, called by writers Campanula Persicifolio, Bells with the peach leafe.
They are common enough, and grow easily in good mold, and are of two colors, the one with a WHITE flower, the other with a BLEW, both single.
They flower in May & June & July.
They are easily encreast from the dividing of their rootes, and are best planted betimes in the Spring, though Autumne will serve. They serve well for dressing up potts.

SAPONARIA

Soapewort, that with the DOWBLE BLUSH *colour is onely esteem'd, which is fulsomely sweet.* The greene leaves and branches dye downe to the ground yearly, but the roote continues, and spreads too much for a little garden. It is best divided and planted about Michelmas, though most tymes of the yeare will serve the turne. It is very hardy. It is in flower in July.

HESPERIS, Rockett

or the Queenes Gilliflower, beareth a stalke full of very sweet Dowble White Flowers in MAY, and requires good earth, and to stand in a warme place abroad all wynter, otherwise to be kept in potts. The leafe is of a darke color, with teeth in the edges like a saw. The flowers grow many on a stalke like stockes, but closer together. Their color is either white or Red, and their sent in hott yeares and countreys very sweet. Wee plant the rootes in the Spring betimes.

OF FIBROUS RANUNCULES

Wee have the Dowble White, *called in Latine Ranunculus Nemorosus plenissimus albus.* In some parts of England it is called Queenes May, and Dowble May, and is not very common. The greene leaves dye yearly before wynter, and spring up againe in the end of February or beginning of March. The roote lives well abroad all wynter, and may bee planted either about

Michelmas, or betimes in the Spring. The flower is like a great dowble daisy.

Then wee have the great dowble YELLOW Globe Crowfoote, whose flowers turne their leaves inwards, and the Little dowble Yellow Erect kind, and a PURPLE dowble Wood Ranuncule is spoken and written of, but I have not seene it.

All flower in Aprill, and are kept in gardens easily, and encreast by dividing their rootes betimes in Spring, if you can find them, or in September.

HOLLYHOCKES

The plant is a kind of MALLOWES, *and therefore called in Latine Malua Rosea, the Mallow Rose. The leaves are great and round, the stalke somtimes three or four yards high, besett with faire flowers from the middle to the tops.*

Wee have single and dowble of these colors, WHITE, PINKE, BLUSH, CARNATION, CRIMSON, SCARLET, BLOOD RED, almost BLACKE, and pale YELLOW, the Dowble of which last was rais'd by the Duke of Orleans in France.

They flower in July and August.

The leaves dye downe with the stalkes yearly, but the rootes continue long in a good rich soyle, and a warme place. The plant is fittest for courts or spatious gardens, being soe great and stately.

Wee encrease them either from Rootes in the fall, or Spring, or from their seed sowne in the Spring which produces new sorts.

CYSTUS

in English the Holy Rose, or the SAGE ROSE, *because the leafe of the plant is somwhat like a sage leafe, wooly and light greene. There are many kinds, but wee esteeme these most:*

CYSTUS LEDON, the Sweet Cystus, with Laurell leaves, and single WHITE flowers, with purple bottomes.

The MALE Cystus, with the great longish leafe, and SINGLE PURPLE flowers with yellow chives, without sent.

The MALE narrow leav'd Cystus, with the YELLOW BLOSSOME.
The FEMALE CYSTUS, with the sage leafe, and WHITE flowers.
They flower in JUNE & JULY.
They are somewhat tender, and hardly scape our wynters, except they bee rais'd of seed, which comes out of Italy, and then not without care and housing. Sow the seed in potts in ye Spring.

ALOE

This is that great greene plant consisting only of long strong pointed leaves that have their sides indented like the sword fish, and are hung up by many to the seelings of their roomes.
There are TWO KINDS *of it:*

The Common Aloes, with the Whitish flowers.
The American Aloes, with the violet colour'd flowers.
They flower in Autumne.
The later kind is very tender, and must bee carefully hous'd in Frosty weather. It is encreast only here by sprouts.

PRIMROSES & COWSLIPS

Both called in Latine VERBASCULA *and* PRIMULAE VERES, *and* PARALYSES *as being good for the Palsey. They are much alike in their greene leafe, but differ more in their flowers, but they are both soe common with us as I shall not describe them.*

There is but one sort of Primrose with a dowble flower, which is of a creame color & sweet, but common. Of the single sorts besides the common Creame color *wee have* many sorts of Red or Purple, amongst which wee account the deepest Red the best, and a pure White which is well esteem'd and a Greene.
Of Cowslips *wee have* also severall differences, some having onely single flowers, others two, one growing out of the other, but all POLYANTHES, that is many on a stalke. Some are YELLOW, some GREENE, some PURPLE OF GRIDELINE, paler & deeper, and some ORENGE, or rather SCARLET, which is not common.

The chiefe tyme of the flourishing of the Cowslips is in MARCH, but the Primroses beginn even in the snowes and frosts of wynter, and continue till May and longer.

They love a good garden mold, and a warme place. Commonly wee set them on the edges of borders, but those of the North or West are better for them than the South or East, for they flourish most in the warme shade.

They may bee encreast at any tyme from their rootes, and sowing their seed as soone as 'tis ripe, or in the Spring, which often brings some new sorts.

DOWBLE WILD PELLITORY, or Sneeswort

Ptarmica silvestris flore pleno in Latine. The flower is small & thicke like a daysy, of a gold yellow colour, the greene leafe shines. It beares in Aprill and grows without trouble in gardens.

DOWBLE FEAVERFEW

hath a dowble white flower like a daisy, growing many of them on high stalkes from one roote.

It beares flowers all sommer and groweth easily in our gardens. It is called in Latine Parthenium flore pleno.

PELLITORY of SPAINE, in Latine also Pyrethrum

Hath a White daisy like flower, with a little yellow thrum in the middle, and greene leaves like fennell.

It flowers in JULY & AUGUST.

HEDYSARUM CANADENSE, French Honysuckle

A kind of Vetch which came first to France from Canada, bearing in May & June many small peach color blossomes set thicke together on the stalke, after which succeed long indented Seed cods, with good seed, from which wee encrease the kind, for the roote seldome lives two wynters here, and therefore it may rather bee accounted Annuall.

EVERLASTING PEASE

It hath a good peach color flower, and is in most things like to other Pease. The Latine name is LATHYRIS NARBONENSIS *latifolius.*
Wee plant this against a warme wall, both because the stalkes must bee supported and tyde up, and that the roote is tender. It is best encreast from the seed. It flowers in MAY & JUNE.

OROBUS VENETUS sive PANNONICUS

is another kind of Everlasting Pease, or rather Vetch, with BLEW *flowers.* It beares in JUNE.

LIMONIUM RAWOLFII SYRIACUM

It hath long deeply indented leaves, which feele rough or hairy. The flowers are many and small, set thicke together, of a pale BLEW *colour, with lesser* WHITE *flowers growing out of them.*
They continue long without fading, and make a pretty, odd shew.
It flowers in June, and most of the sommer afterwards.

TREE HOUSE LEEKE

Sedum Maius arborescens in Latine. It hath fatt iucy leaves, small indented, and set thicke together which are shapt like a tongue, the stalkes strong and high, the flowers yellowish, spredd abroad like little starrs, the seed is blacke and small.
It flowers in IANUARY and FEBRUARY.
This plant is very tender of frosts, yet delights in moysture, and is kept by some in a pot without holes in the bottome, that the water may not passe away.

OF HELLEBORES

Wee have these principall sorts of them:

The True HELLEBORE with the BLACKE Roote and the large WHITE flower, like a single Rose, somtimes dasht with a little red about the edges, with many pale yellow threads standing about a

greene head in the middle of the flower. The leaves are thicke and fatt & great & indented, and of a deepe greene color. The stalkes are many, and rise directly out of the earth.
It flowers in December and IANUARY.

The Great WHITE HELLEBORE with whitish greene starr flowers, many on a stalke like Hyacinthes, and large pale greene leaves finely plaited & ribbed, very beautifull to behold.
The leaves spring out of the earth in March and the Flowers come in IUNE.
This last is somwhat tender, yet it lives all wynter abroad in good mold, and in a warm place.

The LESSER EARLY WHITE HELLEBORE, with deepe Red flowers, whose leaves are like the former, but smaller and lesse beautifull. They come up in February, and the flowers in JUNE.

HELLEBORINE

There are two sorts of it, the one with the greater broader leafe which wee call Our Ladyes Slipper, from the shape of the flower, which is of one sort YELLOW, with fower little purple wynges, of another PURPLE, with fower whyte wynges. The other kind hath many small flowers shapt like that of Satyrium, somtimes purple, somtimes whyte, and sometimes whyte dasht with red. The greene leaves of all the sorts are ribbed like Plantane leaves, and something resembling the leaves of the White Hellebore, but lesse, which occasioned these plants to bee called Helleborines.
The SLIPPER flowers in June, and the other Helleborines a little sooner.

THE BLEW or PURPLE MARIGOLD

Is a kind of ASTER *or Starrwort, called in Latine commonly* ASTER ITALORUM, *the Italian Aster. The leaves and blossome are in figure like our common Marygold.* It blowes in August, and is a pretty plant and growes easily abroad all yeare. It is usually encreast from the roote.

GNAPHALIUM AMERICANUM

American Cottonwort, or Everlasting of America, growes two or three foote high, and hath long narrow leaves up to the tops of the stalkes, where the flowers grow in clusters dowble, consisting of many YELLOW *scales, which continue fresh a long tyme after they are gathered, and wither not away.*
It flowers in August, and is tender.

HARES FOOTE, or LAGOPUS

There is a greater sort and a smaller, they have both leaves growing by threes, and are therefore esteem'd by writers in the number of Trefoiles. The flowers grow at the tops of the branches, in long spikes thicke and close set together.
The greater sort hath flowers of a shining BLOOD RED or Crimson color, and the lesser of a worse paler RED.
They flower in July and August, and are kept easily all yeare abroad in gardens, and encreast from the rootes in AUTUMNE.

SNAPDRAGON

is a common plant growing in Gardens, yet having a beautifull flower, I cannot omit it.
Some have WHITE *flowers, some* RED, *and some* RED *stript with* WHITE.
They flower in MAY & JUNE, and are easily encreast from the rootes in Autumne.

SOLANUM, or Nightshade

I shall say nothing here of Solanum Halicacabum or the Wynter Cherry, nor of other Solanums, but shall only mention here this Deadly or Sleepy Nightshade, with great broad darke greene leaves, and hollow bell flowers, of a Dead PURPLE *color, after which succeed blacke shining berryes, like little cherryes.*
The Italians call this plant Bella Donna, the faire Ladye.
It flowres in the end of the Spring, and most part of the sommer.

HELYCHRYSUM, Golden Life Everlasting, or Moathwort

There are three espetiall kinds of it; one called often in Latine STECHAS CITRINA LUTEA ANGUSTIfolia, the narrow leav'd Stechas, with Yellow scaly tufts, which keepe long without withering, and with whitish narrow wooly leaves.
Another with a broader leafe, sometimes called the broad leav'd Yellow Amaranthus.
They flower in IUNE and IULY.
Coma Aurea is another sort, whose leaves are iagged like Southerwood, and Flowers scaly, and of a shining Yellow color, remaining long soe.
It flowers in AUGUST and SEPTEMBER.

OF DAISYES

I shall only tell you there are about 7 or 8 sorts of Dowble Daisyes with the same greene leafe, but differing in the color of the flowers, & something in the greatnes. They are commonly all WHITE *or* CARNATION *or* CRIMSON *or variegated with White and Red.*
Some of the sorts are proliferous. There is also a GREENE Daisy, and a BLEW one called of ye Alpes. They flower most part of the sommer, and end of the Spring, the Deepe Crimson & the Pinke latest.
They live easily, and encrease extreamly at the rootes.

DOWBLE LADY SMOCKE

In Latine Cardamine flore pleno. The flowers are of a yellowish white color.
It flourisheth in APRILL and MAY, and is easily encreast from the rootes in the Spring or Fall, and lives all wynter abroad.

SWEET WILLIAM

Hath many long strong single stalkes, with many little flowers like

pinkes at the top of them together, some of which are red and some white mixt with red.
This is common and flowereth in JUNE.

MARSH MARIGOLD

In Latine Caltha Palustris. It hath a large roundish veined leafe somwhat indented or notch'd but not much, of a pleasant greene color. The stalkes are green, fatt and strong. The flowers consist of five or six larger outward leaves, and a great many small inner leaves, like some of the Plush Anemones, of an Orenge Yellow color. The leaves continue greene all wynter.
It flowers in the Spring when the Crowfeete doe, and somtimes in ye Sommer.

OF COLOMBINES, Aquilegia

They are common in England & of severall sorts, some with iagged dowble tufted flowers, some of a white color, others blew or red or party color'd with white and purple. Some are dowble, others single.
They flower in May & June, and are easily encreast from seed or rootes.

Wee are now come to the last sort of FIBROUS FLOWERS, *which wee call* ANNUALLS, *because they live but one Sommer, perishing every wynter with the frosts or otherwise, and being perpetuated onely by their seed, which most yield here plentifully and good.*

OF ANNUALLS

Some of the BEAUTIFULLEST SORTS *of Annualls shall here bee spoken of, the rest, which are very many, wee shall not meddle with.*

ADONIS

Hath leaves like Fennell or Mayweed. The flowers are SINGLE, *but of a rich Orient Red, encompassing a darke greene head.* This flowreth in MAY, IUNE, and IULY, and is common in our gardens.

AFRICANS

Or FRENCH *Marigolds, wee have severall diversityes,* as a Greater and a Lesser Dowble, both of an Orenge color, and a Great Single with Yellowish Flowers, and a Lesser Single with Orenge. They flower in the later Sommer moneths.
Sow the seed, which is long blacke and flatt in March betimes, if you will have good seed on a hott bed. The plant is somewhat tender.

ALCAEA

Marsh Mallowes, the best kinds are

That of VENICE, called also in Latine Malua horaria, because it opens in the heate of the day, and closes towards evening, and opens no more. The stalkes are long, round and weake, the leaves large and iagged and divided into three parts. The flowers are large also and beautifull, whitish upwards with purple bottomes and yellow pestles. The seed is blacke, contain'd in rough bladders.
The seed is to be sowne betimes on a hott bed to procure good seed, otherwise in the end of APRILL or May.

That of AMERICA, called also the THORNY MALLOW, and SABDARIFA. The flowers are like the Venetian kind, consisting of five leaves. The seed is like that of Abutilon but greater. It is very hardly rais'd in our countrey from the seed, being a plant that ill endures cold mornings.

That of EGYPT, the flowers grow to the sides of the stalkes, and are yellowish, the seed is downy, & contain'd in long five corner'd vessells, hairy and pointed.
All the sorts flower in the Sommer moneths, and are not common in our countrey.

AMARANTHE

All the Amaranthes (but one) have good large long leaves of a light yellow greene color, broad below, sharpe towards the point, soft to handle and slippery. That other hath the leaves very beautifully markt with three colors, red, greene and yellow. The flowers are onely long spikes of silke as it were, soft and like plumes of feathers generally, but some grow short and thicke together and have some resemblance of a cockes Combe.

When Gerard wrote his Herball, hee knew onely of two PURPLE Amaranthes and one Scarlet, and that with the pointed leaves, but of late yeares the English Florists have rais'd above half a score of new varietyes out of seed that came first from Surat in Persia, many of which are very fine, and are of different scarletts and other reds, or of lovely Yellowes, all the colours very Orient and faire. The stalkes are long and strong and brancht.

They flower all IUNE, IULY and AUGUST, and sometimes longer till the frosty mornings nipp them.

These Amaranthes delight extreamly in the SUN, and must bee sowen betimes in March in fine earth on a hott bed, to get early plants that may perfect their seed before the cold dewes come. The yong plants must bee cover'd and kept from cold wynds till they are very strong. It is tyme enough to sow in Aprill or the beginning of May without a hott bed, if you desire not good seed but the flowers only. The seed is blacke and shining, and must bee sowne as other fine tender seedes are appointed to bee. It is usuall to remove the yong plants twice, first out of the hott bed, as soone as they have little leaves into a bed that hath beene hott, or into some fine rich earth that may bee cover'd, and from thence againe, when they are neere halfe a foote high into other good mold, either in beds or potts, where they must stand to flower.

SCARLET BEANE

In Latine Phaseolus Americanus. This groweth like other Phaseoli or kidney beanes, not well without a wall or other supporters. The leaves grow by threes, and are in shape something like the Ivy leaves. The flowers are like pease blossomes of a fine bright red colour, almost scarlet. The seed is contain'd in Codds as other beanes, and is a large kidney beane of a fine spotted purple color.

It flowreth all sommer almost.

This (as all annualls) is only encreast from seed. Set the beanes in March & Aprill.

BASTARD SAFRAN

CARTHAMUS *Sativus & CNICUS in Latine. It is a kind of Thistle with strong high stalkes, with prickly sharpe pointed leaves, but broad at the bottomes. On the tops of the stalkes stand heads or knobbs with prickly scales, out of which come many silkes or twisting threads of a fine Orenge or* SAFRON *color, which make the flower, and show very beautifully. The seed is White, long and somwhat corner'd.*

It flowers in JULY and AUGUST, and is hardy and easily rais'd from the SEED.

CONVOLVULUS

In Latine also SMILAX, *and in English* BINDWEED, *whereof there are many sorts, some smooth, some hairy, some with small White or Blew flowers, some with larger, but all with such weake stalkes that they need supporters to climb up by.*

The BEST kind is that with great full leaves towards the bottomes but pointed, not cut into three parts as some of the other sorts are. The Flowers are Large, of a good BLEW colour, they are shapt like bells with wide open mouthes. The flower consists onely of one entire undevided leafe, but hath five broad purplish veines or ribbs. Three of these flowers grow commonly neere together, but upon severall short stalkes comming out of another stalke about a handbreadth long.

The seed is blacke about the bignes of Tares.

There is another pretty kind, lesse than the former, with a longish leafe, and Flowers of three colors, that is White in the bottome, Yellow in the middle, and perfect AZURE above.

They flower in most of the sommer moneths.

The seed must bee sowen in Aprill or May in good mold, and the plants set in a warme place against some pillar or rayle or wall.

CORNE FLOWER

in Latine CYANUS, *there are severall sorts single and dowble.*

The Dowble are only a BLEW and a PURPLE. The Single are BLEW, PURPLE, WHITE and stript. Most of the sorts are very common, and grow amongst the corne in the fields, and the Blew is in many places called the Blew Bottle, but there is one sort which came from Constantinople, and is very SWEET and Dowble, of a reddish Grideline color. Wee call it the SWEET SULTAN or the SULTAN's flower, in Latine CYANUS FLORIDUS TURCARUM. This sort is somwhat tender.

All the sorts flower from May till Harvest.

GOATES BEARD

In Latine and Greeke TRAGOPOGON. *Wee have* a PURPLE flower'd, a YELLOW and a BLEW. The seed is long and downy.

They flower from IUNE to AUGUST.

HAWKESWEED

In Latine Hieracium. There are severall sorts with single and dowble Yellow flowers, but that most esteem'd is the APULIAN Hawkes-weed with the BLUSH colour'd flower.
They beare most part of sommer.

LARKE SPURR

In Latine DELPHINIUM *and* CONSOLIDA REGALIS. *Wee have now great varietyes of Larke Spurrs, both single and dowble, with a heele and without, or with a very short one. They are of all these colours, viz.:* VIOLET, PURPLE, BLEW, ASH COLOUR, LEAD COLOUR, WHITE, PINKE, BLUSH, TAWNEY, *and stript or markt with two or three of these colors.* There is a pretty dowble sort like a Rose, variegated with Violet colour and White, and another with Flesh color and Murrey.
Some kinds grow two or three yards high, and have the stalkes set so thicke with flowers that the stalkes are not to bee seene.
They FLOWER all the SOMMER.
The seed is usually sowed in Aprill and May, but it is well sowen also in the end of sommer, quickly after the seed is ripe, for it will live all wynter as many annualls will till they have yielded seed. That which is sowne in the end of sommer will flower betimes in the Spring, and have greater spikes of flowers and more dowble than that sowne at the beginning of the yeare.

INDIAN CRESSES, or NASTURTIUM

Thatt which I shall mention here is Nasturtium Indicum, with the YELLOW *flow'r, on the inside whereof is a Crosse of a deepe* ORENGE *colour, and on the backe a spurr greater and longer than the Larkes spurr.*
It flowers in the heate of Sommer.
The seed is best sowed betimes on a hott bed.

BELLEVEDERE

An Italian name in use, the Latine name is OSYRIS. *It is a kind of* LINARIA *or* FLAX. *It hath many small light greene leaves, and all branches growing from the roote, and shewes like a little Dwarfe Cypresse tree. The beauty is only in the figure of the bush and the leaves, for the flower is very small, and passes away almost undiscerned.*

It is planted in borders along walkes for an ornament in the sommer moneths, and must bee sowne in Aprill or May.

MOATH MULLEINES

Blattaria, the Annualls have some White or Greyish, others Yellow flowers. The seed is small & leafe large.

They flower in IULY and AUGUST.

MOLUCCA

Sweete Balme, there is one kind that is rough or prickly with very pale red flowers and very sweet, and another smooth and without sent.

They flower in IUNE and IULY.

PULSATILLA

Is a kind of wild Anemone, commonly rais'd by us from seed, like bells in shape and hairy without. One sort hath a bright purple flower with a yellow thrumm in the middle. Another hath a white flower.

They flower about EASTER.

This is not an Annuall, but because it is usually rais'd from seed it passes here.

SCABIOUS

The Indian Scabious is that which affords the most beautifull flowers, which are purple with white threads and pendant. The seeds are starry, the leaves large and iagged.

It flowers in IULY and most of the sommer.

It will live sometimes two yeares, if sowne late, and some have the flowers of a lighter red, some of a deeper. The seed will produce variety of colors.

There is a pretty Mountaine Scabious with White flowers, and broad leaves like those of the Primerose.

SONCHUS LANATUS

The Wooly Sow Thistle, one hath a Yellow flower, the other a Blew.
They flower in IUNE and IULY.

VENUS LOOKING GLASSE

with many small weake stalkes, which quickly fall to the earth, and little longish indented leaves, and very pretty violet-colour'd flowers, which stand open all day, and have white threads in their middle, which make a handsome shew. They fade presently.
It flowers in IUNE and IULY.

FOX GLOVES

Digitalis in Latine. The YELLOW *and the* WHITE *are rarest, but the most esteem'd is that which is called in Latine Ferrugineus Digitalis, of a* RUSTY IRON *colour.*
The seed is small & Browne.
They flower in IUNE and IULY.

COVENTRY BELLS

VIOLA MARIANA *have large long hairy leaves like Buglosse, and long neckt bell fashion'd flowers, cut in five parts on the brimms, with whitish chives and downy haire in them. There are with* PURPLE *flowers, and with* WHITE.
They flower in the sommer moneths, and often live two yeares till they have borne seed.

THE WONDER of PERU

Hath leaves like to pescods leaves, and flowers in shape like to those of Tobacco or Convolvulus. On the same roote you shall have together RED, YELLOW *and* WHITE *flowers, and many stript with these colours, very delightful to behold and sweete.*

They shut in the sun.
It flowers from IULY till OCTOBER.
The plant is preserv'd all wynter with great care, but passeth for an Annuall because usually rais'd every yeare from seed, which is of the bignes of pepper.

LUPINES

Wee have of Annuall Lupines one with Yellow flowers, another White, another with small Blew, but the best is the GREAT BLEW. All which flower plentifully all the sommer moneths, and are rais'd in May from the seed which is a kind of Vetch or Pease.

THLASPI CRETICUM, or CANDYTUFTS

The plant exceeds not a foote and a halfe in height. The stalkes are from the bottome brancht into many small branches, and beare at the tops many small flowers, which are somtymes white only, somtymes white spotted with purple, and somtymes also reddish purple. The seed is reddish, like to TREACLE *Mustards. The roote is hard & small, the leaves long and narrow, and of a light greene color, a little notcht upwards.*
It flowers in IUNE and IULY.

OF SHRUBS and TREES us'd for ORNAMENTS of GARDENS

Having briefly spoken of all the sorts of Choice Flowers which wee at present are acquainted with in England, and wherewith wee not only beautify our gardens, but our chambers, and even hands, it remaines that a worthy mention bee made of such Trees and Shrubbs as are conducing also to our pleasure, either in delighting our eyes with the beauty of their leaves or flowers, or their Novelty, or our Smell with the sweetnes or other oddnes of their sents.
And these wee will distinguish into TWO SORTS, *that is to say such as* LOOSE *their* LEAVES *every* WYNTER, *and such as keepe all, or a great part, the whole yeare, and are usually called by us* GREENES, *but wee shall speake of none of either of the two kinds that may not bee admitted into our Gardens or Walkes.*
They whose LEAVES FALL *away every wynter are also of* TWO SORTS; *some of them are not able, by reason of the weaknes of their stems, to grow without supporters, and are usually called* CLIMBING PLANTS; *and some are strong enough to grow of themselves and are therefore tearm'd by Florists* ERECT, *which nevertheles for more heate or ornament are often set against walls or palissades.*

OF CLIMBING SHRUBBS

Wee have three in chiefe Esteeme, viz. the CLEMATIS, *the* WOODBIND, *and the* IASMYNE.

OF the CLEMATIS

The Clematis is a Trefoile, the Leaves growing by threes upon these I mention here.

Wee have these differences

The SINGLE with the RED flower.
The BLEW or PURPLE as some call it with the single flower.
And the DOWBLE DARKE BLEW or PURPLE, this, as the rest, hath the flowers consisting of a Crosse of 4 leaves, but this crosse

here beares up very many small narrow leaves, growing thicke together.

All these flower in IULY and AUGUST.

There is another sort of Clematis, differing in many things from the former, for the leaves are greater of this, and grow by paires, and are of the shape of the Asclepias leafe. This also grows not above a yard high at most, whereas the other run up nine or ten foote, and this dies downe to the roote every wynter.

It is called CLEMATIS PANNONICA, the Hungarian Clematis, and hath a Blew flower, consisting of fower wyngs turning the points up like some daffodills or Jounquilles, and a head or cup within consisting of a thrum of pale yellow threads. It hath no smell, and is espetially called a Clematis from the hot biting tast of the leaves. It flowers in May or June.

They are all encreast by sproutes or layers from the old rootes remov'd in October, or thereabouts.

They love a warme place and good earth.

OF WOODBINDS

The Woodbind or Honysuckle is called in Latine PERYCLYMENUM and CAPRIFOLIUM.

Wee have besides the common wild sort, two others very sweete, which are

The Great YELLOW ITALIAN kind, called in Latine Perfoliatum, because the stalkes passe through the leaves. The flowers grow in two heights.

And the little RED Woodbind, called by some the Spanish Woodbind.

These beginn to flower in Aprill, but the Red last, and continue most part of the sommer.

A loose earth, somwhat sandy agrees best with woodbinds, and any place, either hot or shady.

They are easily encreast by sproutes or cuttings, and endure well all weathers abroad.

Wee have severall kinds of Jasmyns, differing from one another both in the Leaves and flowers.

The First is the COMMON JASMYN, with the small single white flower, consisting of five leaves, very sweet. The stalkes are long, round, branched, and (when yong) very greene without & white within. The leaves stand one against the other, are long, narrow, and of a darke greene. The seed is said to bee flat and broad like Lupines, but it cometh not to perfection in England. This kind runneth up very high, and spreads much against walls, and is the proper stocke to graft or enoculate the other sorts of Jasmyns upon.

It flowers from the end of May most part of the heate of sommer.

This is hardy enough to live abroad with us all wynter without covering, if it stand against a South or East wall, and bee well shelter'd from nipping winds, otherwise the upper part of the branches will dye every wynter, which must hinder the Flowring the next sommer. It loves a soyle warme and light and not wett, and is easily encreast by sproutts or layers, which take presently at any part of the branch, and are best remov'd about Michelmass, though the Spring also will serve.

Then wee have the SPANISH JASMYN, otherwise called the CATALONIAN, which is very like the former in the leaves, but hath larger flowers, which are White all but the bottomes, which are reddish. This is but a Dwarfe in respect of the other, not growing usually much above a yard high, with weake branches. The flowers are more strongly sweete, and soe make better Essence in hot countreys. This flowers later than the common sort, and is soe tender that wee hardly preserve it all wynter in potts or tubbs, yet in Paris, where the frosts are sharper than in England, I have seene a south wall planted with this kind, enoculated upon the common white, which in October were unnayl'd and layd downe upon the earth, and a low wall of horse dung, or what else you please made before them to keepe off the cold, covering them well with mosse, and a penthouse of boards to keepe off the snow and great raines, leaving places to give them some ayre in fine wynter weather, letting them lye thus till the great frosts of wynter are past, and then removing all the covers, and pruning them low, and nayling the stockes up againe to the walls, where they bore flowers abundantly in sommer.

Betimes in the Spring before the Spanish kind begins to bud, you must every yeare, prune them close downe to the stocke, leaving not soe much as one eye above it, unles it bee a branch of a finger long of new sprouting for a graft, and, by the way, note that these come better of grafts than enoculation, or any other way of insition. If they bee not yearly pruned thus low, to force out now branches, they will bee but shortlived. When it begins to freese in the house, take your potts or tubbs into the roome you keepe them in all wynter, opening the windows in faire weather, and watering them a little with water that hath stood in the ayre or sun, or such as the dishes and vessells in the kitchen have beene washed withall, but not hott nor warme, and taking great care that you never touch the stemme of the tree, nor the branches with the water in watering.

Remove them early in the Spring, or about the middle of September, and when you cutt off the dead tops, cover them with softened wax to keepe out the frosts or March wynds.

They use sometymes to barbe the rootes when they have stood long, & then put new mold to them, rich, yet light and warme, not too moist. Water this kind often in sommer if the season bee dry.

In Italy they have amongst the curious in some places a Dowble White Jasmyn of this Spanish kind, but I conceave it only made soe by pruning and force of culture, which causeth the roote to dye quickly, and that there is no such constant kind.

THE ARABIAN OR ALEXANDRIAN Jasmyn, called in Italian Gelsimeno del Gime, is another kind of Jasmyn with white flowers, somwhat Dowble, with not above ten leaves at most, extraordinary sweete, surpassing any of the other Jasmyns, as partaking both of the sent of the Orenge and Jasmyn flowers. It hath leaves like the White Syringa, but not indented and thinner and paler, standing in pairs oppositely, and somwhat resembling the Orenge leaves. It is but a Dwarfe shrubb, not growing above a Cubitt or two high, and came first from Egypt, and is called by the Arabians SAMBACH.

It flowers from Aprill even to October.

It is very tender, yet prospereth well in diverse places of Italy, where they have had it long, though it hath not yet beene brought into England to my knowledge.

It is potted and hous'd there in wynter & therefore must necessarily here betymes bee soe too, and taken forth of the house late in the Spring. It is inoculated on the single common white Jasmyn stocke, and pruned low the first yeare, and the succeeding lesse, to keepe it in the shape of a little bush, for it is not set against a wall as the common useth to bee.

Thus much for the White Jasmyns, there are three also with YELLOW *flowers, and one with a kind of* ORENGE, *and these are all the sorts wee are yet acquainted with.*

The chiefest of the Yellow kinds is that which is called the YELLOW INDIAN Jasmyn, whereof wee shall speake in a more proper place, as being a GREENE. Ye flowers are very sweete. Then there is the Dwarfe YELLOW JASMYN, of the nature of the common White, and the Trefoile YELLOW sort with small flowers which have no sent. It is called by writers in Latine Jasminum Luteum bacciferum, and Trifolium fruticans, and Polemonium Monspeliense, and is rather a Broome than a Jasmyn, of little beauty and esteeme, yet kept in many gardens.

It flowreth in the heate of sommer, and groweth without trouble in good mold.

The ORENGE OR SCARLET flowred Jasmyn, called by some the Jasmyn of Canada, by others the purple with the Oblong Codds, by others CORNUTUS, his Ivy Jasmyn, hath many long tubous flowers growing together on many short feete, in shape like a Gentianella, but of a rich Red colour. The leaves are somwhat like the Ashe, but indented, and the stalkes long and weake, and clasping like the Ivyes.

It flowers most part of SOMMER.

This is hardy enough, growing abroad all wynter, in ye gardens against walls, but a South or East wall is requisite.

It loves a rich earth, and much watering from the end of Spring till the approach of Wynter, delighting in warmth & moysture.

It is encreast either by sprouts, layers, or the seed with us, without any great difficulty, & by some by cuttings also.

Besides these PERENIALL there is one ANNUALL Jasmyn, called by diverse names as QUAMOCLIT, the AMERICAN RED JASMYN, the Exoticke CONVOLVULUS, & the Jasmyn with the leafe of the Millefolium, which is very narrow, and deepely cutt. The flowers are longish and tubous, open at the mouths, divided into five parts, of a color like red wax, with long pale tamyns, and without any sent. The stalkes run up high, and must bee supported.

It flowers in August & September.

Sow the seed in May or June at furthest, and gather them before they bee very ripe, otherwise they are in danger of being lost. This plant is very tender.

OF ERECT SHRUBBS and TREES, which need no support

It was sayd before these are distinguisht into TWO SORTS, *such as loose their Leaves yearly, and such as* EVER KEEPE *them, and are therefore called by us* GREENES.

Of the FIRST SORT *I shall only make choice of the* PRINCIPALL *which are the* ROSE, *the* MEZEREUM, AGNUS CASTUS, ALTHAEA, GOATES

RUE, AZEDERACH, FRAXINELLA, SYRINGA, CYTISUS, COLUTAEA, *the* POMEGRANATE *Tree*, LABURNUM, JUDAS TREE, *the* SWEET OLIVE, *the* VIRGINIAN BAY, *the* PERSIAN JASMYN, HYPERICUM ARBORESCENS, ACACIA, TRAGACANTHA, *the* LILAC, AMOMUM PLINII, *the* TREE OF LIFE, *the* TAMARISKE, CHRISTS THORNE.

OF ROSES

I begin with the SWEETEST *and Loveliest, in all ages cherished and esteem'd. Some are* SINGLE *kinds, and some* DOWBLE.

None of the *Single* are much valued by us except the Sweet Brier, for the sent of its leaves, and the Scarlet Rose, which is Yellow within, and Scarlet on the outside. It hath the small leafe of the Yellow kind, and weake branches of a red colour. It is but a Dwarfe, and is therefore usually enoculated on a Damaske or PROVINS, and because of the weaknes of the branches is usually set against a wall or palissade. It is a great bearer, but the flowers fall quickly. It loves a warme station, and agrees not with clipping or other pruning than to take away dead spriggs.
It flowers with the other kinds.

OF DOWBLE ROSES there are REDS, WHITES and YELLOW, and some stript or variegated with TWO COLOURS.

The DEEPEST REDS *are*

The VELVET Rose, of a deepe MURREY OR PURPLE color, with some yellow thrums in the middle. The leaves are darke greene and spotted in some places with Red, somwhat larger than those of the common Red Rose. The prickles on the branches are very small, and may bee handled without offense. The flowers are not above two or three heights of leaves, which are large, and lye spreadd open. It growes up to a good high bush, and beares in standards very well, but the flowers last not. It abounds in succours at the Roote.
The PURPLE Rose, bearing a faire flower, but not soe great as

the Provins, composed of very many small leaves set thicke together, and shewing no seeds in the middle. The color is deeper than the common Red, but not soe sad as the Velvet Rose. The leaves are like those of the Red. It growes to a competent height, and beares well, and is esteem'd for its dowblenes and scarcity as much as any rose wee have. It may bee kept in standards, but is most usually planted against a wall.

The PURPLE stript with WHITE, about Norwich, very rare.

The Common RED Rose, of an ill faded Red colour, and too few leaves. It is commonly kept low in a hedge, but will grow reasonable high.

The MARBLED Rose, hath the leafe of the Common Red, the flower is thicke & close enough, of the colour of the Common Red, bespotted or full speckled with an ill faded white. It is a great bearer, and usually set in standards.

ROSA MUNDI or the Christmass Rose, another new stript or variegated rose, first found in Norfolke a few years since, upon a branch of the common Red Rose, and from thence multiplied. It is like the Red in all things, but that it is stript in great flakes with indifferent good White.

The CINNAMON, a pretty sweet little Rose, very thicke, with redd branches, and small weake thornes. It is very common, and therefore no more of it here.

The GREAT RED PROVINS, with little sent, called now Centifolia Inodora in Latine, and formerly of Plyny Rosa Campana. It hath great leaves sett by paires thinne on the stemms, of a lighter color than those of the common Red, and growes into a tall bush, and loves not to bee kept low. It stands best against a wall, as the other great thicke flower'd Roses doe, yet beares in Standards.

The HUNGARIAN Rose, of an ill faded Red, fit only for stockes to enoculation, it growing high and lusty.

The ROSE without THORNES, of a color betwixt a Red and a Damaske, and SWEET.

Of the PALER REDS *are*

The DAMASKE Rose, very common with us, though it bee the sweetest of all, of a carnation color, indifferent full of leaves. It growes high in standards well, and hath paler and greater leaves than the Red.

The VARIEGATED DAMASKE, or YORKE AND LANCASTER, which is the true Damaske, striped well with White, a fine Rose when it markes rightly, sweet as the Damaske, and no fuller of leaves, called in Latine Prenestina.

The MONTHLY ROSE, a very Damaske in leaves and flower and sent, but it beares two or three moneths more in the yeare than the ordinary Damaske, and very plentifully, if it stand warme. It is called often ROSA ITALICA.

The DAMASKE PROVINS, a very large, and very Dowble Rose, of the color of the Damaske, and somwhat sweete. It hath such leaves as the Red Provins, but of a lighter greene color, and grows high like that. It is often called BATTAVICA MULTIPLEX in Latine.

The SWEET WILD ROSE or BRIER ROSE, not above two or three heights dowble, of a little deeper Red than the Damaske.

OF DOWBLE WHITE ROSES there are the PURE WHITE Dowble, with a weake sent. It growes very high and loves not cutting. Is full of very sharp strong prickles.

The WHITE PROVINS, a very sweete and very thicke Rose, with a little eye of very pale red in it. It beares very many flowers, and continues long, and growes high and strong.

The DOWBLE MUSKE, extreame sweet, the leaves are long and shining greene. It growes high, and hates pruning at the topps, and loves a warme wall or hedge.

Of YELLOW ROSES wee have only one Dowble, which is as bigg as a reasonable Provins, when it blowes well, which it seldome does, either in England or other countreyes, being eaten up commonly with wormes in the bud. In Italy they hold it likes best in a coole place. Wee know by experience that it loves to run up high, and not to bee cut at the tops. It is a lovely flower, being of a rich yellow color. The leafe is very small, and of a shining pale greene color. It blowes very well in open pure aire neere Hogmagog hills, not farr from Cambridge, and a light soyle.

All the kinds abovementioned flower from May to August, but the Monthly Rose beares most part of the yeare, and the Cinnamon early in the Spring, and the Dowble Muske flowers not till the end of Sommer.

These are the sorts of Roses wee have in England, at least the principall, all which prosper in a good rich garden mold, but not wett. They are either encreast by succours, layers, deviding of the rootes, cuttings, graffing, inoculation of seed. In old tyme the seed was ordinarily sowne, but now 'tis left off, it being soe long before it comes to beare, and the other wayes of multiplication soe easy, but the sowing of the seed in great quantityes certainly produces some new differences. The Cuttings are best set in October and November, and then also the Rootes devided, or the succours remov'd, though their rootes may also bee planted betimes in the Spring. Lay the layers about Michelmass, and remove them in the Spring.

All the kinds rather delight in shade than in a hott sun, a meane is best, but the cuttings and layers are best remov'd and set in the shade, and must bee water'd. It is enough to leave two or three eyes or buds above ground when you plant them, cutting off the rest, and every other yeare at furthest prune all the sorts very close, for the yong second yeare branches beare most flowers, and digg the earth about the rootes once or twice a yeare at least, putting old dung to them, and watering them with blood when you have it.

In Italy there hath beene above twenty yeares a fine Rose, the seed whereof came thither from the East Indyes. It is called in Latine commonly ROSA SINENSIS, and by the Indians Fuyo.
It growes to a high tree for a rose, hath a leafe like a figg, or the Ivyes, and dowble large flowers, which at first breaking forth are White, and then turn Carnation, and at last Purple, and last not in Europe above two or three dayes, and in the Indyes but one, yet change into the three severall colors aforesaid in that short tyme. It is not sweet but very beautifull, yet looseth its greene leaves yearly. It is easily encreased either from cuttings or the roote or seed, and is very tender of cold, and therfore must bee hous'd in wynter, and endureth not wett upon the leaves. Hee that desireth a larger description of it, and of its culture may resort to FERRARIUS, who hath written of it, and was the first raiser of it from seed in our parts of the world.
It is in flower in SEPTEMBER.

OF THE MEZEREON TREE

It is called in Latine Mezereum Germanicum, Chamaelea Germanica, and Laureola folia deciduo, the Lawrell with the falling leafe, that is that continues not on the tree all wynter. It hath leaves like the privet, but they are thicker and not soe pointed. The flowers have but fower very small leaves apiece, and break forth of the very wood of the branches as those of the Judas tree doe, before the greene leaves appeare. They are a little sweet, and turne into berryes.

Wee have three SORTS *of this Shrubb*

One with purple or deepe RED flowers,
Another with peach or Paler Red,
And a third with White, which is the least common.
They all flower in February & March.
The shrubb is hardy and growes abroad all wynter without prejudice in good soyle, and is encreast by sprouts and layers.

AGNUS CASTUS, or VITEX

In English the Chast tree, hath long narrow light greene leaves, not indented, growing by Fives as Hempe, with many small BLEWISH PURPLE sweet flowers growing thicke together at the tops of the branches. They blossome in August, and the greene leaves come in May.

It is tender, and must bee hous'd in wynter. Wee encrease it only by layers, lay'd downe in Autumne.

ALTHEA FRUTICOSA

Tree Mallowes, is a small tree, with a hard whitish barke, large, soft, wooly, light greene leaves, sharpe pointed but deeply cutt in on the sides. The Flowers are like the Mallowes, and are either RED or WHITE, and out of the seeds of these two kinds other GRIDELINES and PURPLES have been lately rais'd in England. They flower in AUGUST & SEPTEMBER.

They agree best with a wall, and live abroad all wynter, and are encreast by seed and layers. It is a pretty flowerbearing tree and not common.

FRAXINELLA

Called somtimes Bastard Dittany, and White Dittany. It groweth not above a yard high, or thereabouts, and all the branches which are many and strong, and shoote out directly from the roote, dye downe yearly to the ground againe. The leaves grow like the Ash, from whence it is named Fraxinella, or the little Ash, or rather the Licoras, they are rough and hard & of a darke greene color, and of a resinous smell. On the tops of the branches grow many fayre and lovely flowers, of five leaves, WHITISH and stript with PURPLE. The undermost leafe of the flower hangeth downe low, the other bearing up, and out of the middle cometh a tassell of long haires like a beard turning up at the bottome. The seed is blacke and shining, contained in huskes like Colombines.

There is another sort with a larger and a LIGHTER RED FLOWER, and another with a WHITE, which is best esteem'd.

They come up out of the earth in February and March, and Flower in June and July, and the seed is ripe in August.
The plant groweth abroad all the yeare, and likes a shady place well, and is easily encreast from seed, or parts of the roote with heads on from which branches sprout.

GOATES RUE

In Latine Galega and Ruta Capraria, it hath many long slender weake branches, which sprout from the roote, and must have a wall or palissade to support them. The leaves are long and narrow like those of Tare or wild Vetch. It seldome lives above a wynter or two, and is best encreast by the seed. It growes without trouble in our clymate, and wee have TWO SORTS of it, one with a light BLEW colour'd flower, which is the commoner, and one with a WHITE flower.
It flourisheth in IUNE & IULY.

THE PERSIAN JASMYN

Called often by writers after the Turkish name AGEM LILAC, and by us a Jasmyn for no other reason that I can find out but that the leaves are a little notcht like the common yellow Jasmyn, and the flowers small, for otherwise it hath not resemblance to Jasmyns in generall, the shrubb growing up into a little tree strong enough to become a stander, and not to neede a wall or other support. The leaves are of a sadd greene color, in shape resembling a little to privett. The flowers are pale BLEW, and grow many together on the tops of the branches, very sweet.
It flowreth from APRILL to IULY with us, and in some places againe before wynter.
It will live abroad with us against a warme wall, but is often kept in tubbs or other vessells to bee hous'd in wynter, and is only encreast by layers or sprouts when the tree is old.
It loves a good garden mold. The layers are to bee layd when those of other trees are, which is commonly in the end of

Autumne, and remov'd best also in Autumne, though it may bee done in the Spring.

THE SWEET OLIVE

or TREE *of* PARADISE, *in Latine commonly called* OLEASTER EXOTICUS, *and* BOHEMICUS, hath leaves somwhat like the willow, but whiter and more wooly and soft, in short the same with the other OLIVE. The Flowers are extreame sweet, of the shape of little short hyacinthes, and of a faded yellowish greene color. The boughes have some thornes on them, the Tree grows to a good height.

It beareth flowers in May.

The tree is reasonable hardy, yet beareth with us most and sweetest flowers against a wall, where it may have roome to run up a good height, else it will not have flowers, nor till it bee of fower yeares growth at least. It is easily encreast by sprouts, layers or cuttings, which take in moist earth and a shady place.

A good rich fatt earth agrees best with the tree, which is not yet common in our countrey.

The POMEGRANATE TREE

Malus Punica in Latine. It grows up to a reasonable high tree, hath narrow shining greene leaves somwhat like the lesser or male mirtle, but greater, and the richest scarlett color'd flowers of any tree or plant. The wild kind hath single flowers, and the other (which is called in Latine BALAUSTIUM) dowble, of the same rich color.

They flower in IUNE & IULY.

In the yeare 1655 a merchant brought a roote of a Balaustium to London out of Italy, which hee affirm'd to bee stript with white and scarlett, but it dyed the same wynter before it bare.

Both the single and dowble kinds are tender, and in England are usually sett in tubbs to bee hous'd in wynter, but the Single I have seene prosper well with us abroad all wynter against a South wall, with care had of it in great frosts.

They both love a rich earth, but not wett, and are best encreast by sprouts & layers.

IUDAS TREE

It growes to the height of a competent tree, hath light greene leaves pointed at the end, and roundish towards the stalke, like the Poplers, they are only one on each stalke. Before the leaves come, the flowers breake out of the wood of the tree, they are shapt like pease blossomes, and grow on short footstalkes, three or fower neere together. The Colour is ordinarily RED, though there is a rare sort with WHITE.

They are in Flower in MARCH.

This tree likes well abroad with us all wynter, yet most plant it against a wall. It is easily rais'd from the seed which is flatt and of a darke red colour, or encreast from sprouts of the roote or layers.

LABURNUM

or ANAGYRIS *in Latine, and Beane Trefoile in English,* because the leaves grow commonly by threes, which are long and smooth. The flowers are of a perfect yellow color, and like those of Broome. Wee have two sorts of Laburnums, one that stinketh nauseously, leaves and flowers, and is kept by the curious for the odnes of the smell, the other hath no sent at all, wee have two kinds of it, one with a broader leafe, the other with a narrower. All the sorts grow up to reasonable high TREES, and grow in standards abroad all the yeare without trouble, and are easily encreast by cuttings or sprouts.

They Flower in May and Iune.

OF THE BASTARD SENA TREE

In Latine COLUTEA, *wee have two* PRINCIPALL SORTS

One called VESICARIA in Latine, because its seed is contained in little thinne bladders, like those in a fish. The tree grows higher than most shrubbs, and hath leaves like Liquorice, or the French

Honysuckle. The Flowers are yellow and Broome like, and become little blacke flatt seeds of the bignes of tares.

The other is called SCORPION SENA, because the seed cases are long & narrow like a Scorpion's tayle. This is like the former much in everything but that it is lesse, and growes not soe high. The seed is long, smooth and browne.

Both these Coluteaes Flower from MAY till sommer bee well spent.

They prosper well in ye gardens all wynter, and are soon rais'd from their seed, and the first is easily encreast by any cutting stucke in a moist earth.

Here by the way I cannot but enforme the Reader that though these Two before mention'd plants are called SENAES, yet they little resemble the TRUE ORIENTALL SENA, which wee use in physicke, for that is rather an hearbe than a shrubb, not above a cubitt high with many slender branches. The leaves are of a yellowish greene colour, pointed, and growe in paires with very short stalkes. The Cods are crooked, flattish and blackish. The plant is very tender, and must bee carefully hous'd in wynter with us, but this by the way.

CYTISUS

Shrub TREFOYLE *or Milk Trefoile is a plant which hath many diversityes of it,* and few of them common in England. They all agree in that they have yellow Broome flowers, and that their leaves stand like Trefoyles by threes, and they differ chiefly in the hairines and smoothnes of the leaves, and the height and smallnes of the shrubbs.

The Principall of the smooth leav'd Cytisi are One with a long leafe, the Other with a Round leafe.

Of the ROUGH or hoary leav'd there is also one with long leaves, which groweth to the height of a man, and one with round, commonly called CYTISUS MARANTHA, from him that first described it. It is called also Cornutus and Lunatus in Latine, from the crookednes of the Codds or cases of the Seed, which is small, flatt and yellowish like broome seed. These flower in MAY and IUNE, but that of Marantha in Autumne in some places.

The last, horned Cytisus is tender and must bee hous'd, the rest harder, and may live under a wall. All are rare in England, and must bee rais'd here from seed, which is to bee had from Italy, for wee have few plants to get succours from.

There are diverse other lesse considerable Cytisi, which I mention not, only one more I shall add, which is called Cytisus Columellae, whose leaves grow by fives, as the other by threes, and whose flowers are whitish with purple tops, growing at the upper ends of the branches, like Melilote. The Cods are browne, and the seed small and round.

OF the LILAC TREE and SYRINGA

It is corruptly called in England the LELAPS by many, and *wee have these varietyes.*

The LILAC with the PALE BLEW Flowers, which is very common.

That with the WHITE flower, very sweete, scarce here.

And that with the RED flower, scarcest of all.

These three sorts grow up to pretty high trees, differing only in the colour of the flowers, which are small and grow many together, but the leafe is alike, which is smooth, soft and shining, like the Ivy.

The other Sort is properly called the Syringa, and often the Italian Syringa. It agrees but little with the former, for it is more a shrubb, and hath a rough barke, the other having a very smooth one, and the edges of the leaves indented like a saw, wh. the other hath not. The flowers are much larger than the other and fulsomely sweet, but with a little smell of the Orenge flower, the other kind rather approaching the Jasmyn. This is common in England, I meane with a single flower, but there is a sort of this shrub in Italy with a dowble flower, which wee have not.

All the sorts flower in MAY or JUNE, but the Italian last of all.

They live abroad all seasons without danger, and are easily encreast from succours, which the last sort casteth out in abundance.

ACACIA

There are Three Sorts of ACACIAES. *One called the* AMERICAN, *the other the* AEGYPTIAN, *and the third is a lesser shrub growing in* PONTUS *and* CAPPADOTIA. I make a great question whether the American and Aegyptian bee not the same, though they are described of writers to differ, espetially in the greatnes and smallnes of the trees, for the Aegyptian is by some sayd to bee but a little shrub in respect of the other, mistaken, I thinke, for that of Pontus, which is soe. The American I have seene in England growe to a high tree, with long narrow even leaves standing but thin on the branches, yet at equal distances, bearing very sweete White flowers in May, but not perfecting seed, which is sayd to come in rough round shells of the bignes of Nutts.

There are some sharpe thornes on the tree here and there, the barke is hard and rough, and the branches brittle.

That of Egypt or Alexandria, for it is called by both names, is said to have yellowish flowers, growing together sphaerically, every one on his stalke, consisting of a soft downish substance, to which succeed Cods like those of the Lupine, containing browne reddish seed, hard and markt like the Tamar rinds with a circle.

The Gumme called Arabicke is had from this tree.

The ACACIA of CAPPADOCIA hath leaves like RUE, and is also thorny.

That of America and Egypt have been rais'd here in England from seed, and the first came to perfection, but the latter have all died the first wynter after they came up, according to my enquiry and intelligence. At that age I saw little difference in the leafe of these two. That of Pontus I have not seene in our Countrey. The American is multiplyed from succours and layers as well as seed, which is best sowne on a hott bed.

It flowers in May with us.

AZEDERACH

It is a fine tree, and yet rare with us, the wood is very hard and the barke rough. The leaves are large, deeply cutt in, of a pleasant greene color. The Flowers are PURPLE.
It blossomes in IUNE.
Wee keepe this yet in tubbs, and house it in wynter, by reason of the hardnes of the wood. It is encreast very difficultly by layers and the seede I have not yet seene.

HYPERICUM ARBORESCENS

It is called in the Duke of Orleans his Catalogue, Hypericum frutescen Americanum flore albo, the Shrub St John's Wort, with the White flower, and by Bauhinus PRUNO SILVESTRI AFFINIS CANADENSIS, that of Canada like the Sloe tree. More I cannot adde, it having fayled much to live in England.

TRAGACANTHA

or SPINA HIRCI MATHIOLI, *or* MASSILIENSIS, *and* POTERIUM, *in right English* GOATES THORNE. It hath many spreading branches beset with long narrow Lentill leaves, and full of very long sharpe hard thornes. The Flowers are small and white. The seed is in little cods like that of Lotus, alias Horned Trefoile, from the roote is got the Gumm Tragacant, or Dragon as it is called corruptly.
It flowreth in the sommer moneths.
It is best encreast by the seed. It keepes on the leaves very often the whole yeare, or till the Spring.
There is another lesser shrub called Tragacantha Rawolfii, prickly like the former with yellow flowers.

THE VIRGINIAN BAY

Hath leaves somwhat like the Lawrell, but lesser and more indented. The Blossomes are small and WHITE, and the berryes blacke when ripe.

Thought to bee THUYA *and* CEDRUS LYCIA. It groweth to the height of a small tree, hath a red barke, and many spreading branches, which hang downe by reason of the smallnes of them, and the weight of the leaves, which are not soe through their largenes (for they are very small like the Savine) but the thickenes & oylines of them. They smell strong and aromatickely. The Flowers are little and yellowish, after which come little cones, like those of the cypresse, with seed in them.

It liveth well abroad all wynter in England in a standard, and is easily encreast by cuttings and sproutes, or layers which take presently.

OF CHRISTS THORNE

In Latine PALIURUS, it is a shrubby bush, with small roundish leaves and many sharpe thornes. The flowers grow in clusters, and are small and of a Yellow colour, which are succeeded by thin flatt seed like flax seed, in hard thin skynny bucklers. It growes plentifully in Palestine, and 'tis thought the crown of thornes was of it.

OF THE TAMARISKE

It growes to a competent height of a tree, hath a red barke, and small narrow leaves like Heath, with small mossy whitish red flowers.

It flowers in MAY.

The tree prospers well in England, enduring abroad well all wynter, and is easily encreast from the roote by sproutes and layers.

AMOMUM PLINII

called by us also corruptly the MUMMY *tree*. It hath many small branches, covered with a light greene barke. The leaves are long and narrow like those of the PEACH but lesse, the flowers are small, white, with a little yellow pointell in the middle, like Garden Nightshade, after which follow small round bright red berryes, like little cherryes, with little flatt yellow seed in them.

It flowers in MAY, and the berryes are ripe in September, which make a good shew with the greene leaves.

This shrubb is but small, but handsome and well esteem'd. It must bee hous'd in wynter, and is encreast by layers and sproutes.

OF GREENES

Wee are now in the last place to speake of GREENES, *that is such Shrubbs and Trees as wee esteeme much, and beautify ye Walkes and Gardens withall, which continue greene all wynter, not casting their leaves totally any season of the yeare.*

The GREATER SORT *of these are the* CEDAR, *the* SCARLET OAKE, *the* FIRRE, *the* PINE, *the* CYPRESSE, *the* YEW, *the* BAY, *the* LAWRELL, *and lastly the* HOLLY, *though common, and most of these grow to bee very Great Trees.*
There is another sort which become also Trees, though not neere soe great as the former, which are the ARBUTUS, *the* ORENGE, *the* LEMMON, *the* CITRON, *the* LAURESTINE, *the* SASAFRAS, *the* PYRACANTHA, *the* PHYLLYREA, *the* ADRACHNE, *the* MOLLE, *and the* CORALL TREE.
The last kind are small and SHRUBBY *such as the* YELLOW JASMYN, MIRTLE, GALE, JUNIPER, RUSCUS, BERRYBEARING SAVINE, *the* OLEANDER, SPANISH BROOME, SPURGE OLIVE, WIDOW WAILE, SESILE AETIOPICUM, BARBA IOVIS, TREE HOUSE LEEKE, ALOE, IUCCA, CAPILLI VENERIS *or Maidenhaires,* COTYLEDONS, *or Navellworts.*

Take first this Generall rule that all Greenes are best remov'd in SEPTEMBER, *that they may get good roote before frosts.*

OF THE CEDAR

The CEDAR TREE usually called of LIBANUS is the esteem'd Speties of Cedars (for there are other lesse valued sorts). It growes in diverse places of Asia to bee the greatest of trees, and hath a very sweet resinous smell. The leaves are small and ever greene, like those of the Larix tree, and not farr unlike to the Juniper. It beareth great Cones like those of the Firr, but larger and not soe pointed, whereon the seed lyes. About each seed there is a sweet oyly substance, very pleasant and Balsamaticall. No tree continues longer free from corruption than this. Wee have of late had some few plants rais'd from seed, which are yet very small, soe that it is rare in England as well as in the rest of Europe. It growes as writers relate Pyramide like, and the boughs hang very orderly, soe it would bee a very lovely tree in Walkes if wee could compasse it, which no doubt may bee done from seed. It would without question prosper well enough with us, for certainly 'tis of the nature of Firrs or Pines, which agree in cold countreys as well as hott, and grow in Asia on the tops of the highest rocky mountaines, such as Mount Libanus, Taurus, and Imaus, which are cover'd with snow in wynters.

The culture of it wee understand not yet, but where it growes naturaly the soyle is stony and dry. There is a small kind called OXYCEDRUS.

THE SCARLET OAKE

In Latine ILEX COCCIGERA, called Scarlet not from the color of the wood, or leaves which are greene at all tymes, but from a certaine excrescence growing to some trees, wherein wormes are bred and a graine of which a perfect scarlet color is made.

The tree produceth acornes as other oakes doe, and groweth very great and high, the leaves are greene above, and grey underneath, snipt about the edges, and prickly at the points. It is a faire lovely tree, frequent in the south parts of France, some few wee have in England, the largest groweth in Whitehall garden.

It is best encreased from the Acornes, and will live all wynter abroad with us.

OF THE FIRR TREE

It is of late yeares well knowne in our countrey, many having beene rais'd from seed to plant in walkes and groves, but certainly long since there were abundance, for many bodyes of Firr trees are found buried in the earth in boggy moorish places in Lancashire, Shropshire and North Wales, as they digg for turfe. This tree grows very handsomely up on high, the branches besetting the body orderly by degrees of heights, and hanging their ends equally downe. The leaves are small, and never fall

away all at a season, they resemble those of the Yew tree, but are of a lighter greene. The seed is contained in Cones like the Pine Apples, and the flowers are but chaffy and small. The finer sort of Firrs wee call Spruce firrs, being brought from PRUSSIA. It growes commonly in very cold clymates and therfore cannot bee in danger in our wynters.
Wee encrease them easily from the seed.

THE PINE TREE

Another Greene fitt for walkes, and groves, growing up to bee a high tree is the PINE, whose leaves are long and pointed, and soe small and narrow that they seeme to bee round like to the stalkes of Spanish Broome. The seed is contained in Cones or hard Cloggs.
It is of the nature of the Firr, and encreast like it best from the seed. There are many sorts of Pines, but wee esteeme that the best called in Latine PINUS SATIVA or DOMESTICA.

OF THE CYPRESSE TREE

Another Tree much us'd by us for Walkes is the CYPRESSE, which, with tying up the many slender branches it casts forth from the roote, and soe along the body pyramide wise, wee make to appeare very beautifull. The leaves are very prickly, narrow and small somwhat like the Tamariske, & smell of Rosin. The seed is in Cones which are smaller than those of the Firr or Pine, from which of late yeares wee encrease this tree very much.
It is hardy enough to endure ye wynters abroad, though somwhat tenderer than the beforementioned greenes.

THE EWE or YEW TREE

This is an old English tree, and is found abroad sometimes in ye woods, but often in our churchyards. It is common and yet I could not omitt it being as good a greene as any of the former.

It growes up to a great tree, having its spreading branches thicke besett with small narrow leaves like Rosemary.
The best way of encreasing it is by sowing the berryes, for the yong trees remov'd hardly grow, no more than the Hollyes doe.

OF THE BAY TREE

This is very common in England and needs no description. It growes to a great tree with us, and lives abroad all wynter, yet it is often nipt, and somtimes killed with great frosts and March wynds, being a tree proper to the hott countreys. It is encreast by slips, succours, or sowing of the berryes. This common but sweet tree is called in Latine Laurus, whereof the Emperors themselves amongst the Romanes wore Garlands.
There is another tree wee have of late yeares seene in England and given the name of the ORENGE BAY to it, because it looks and smells like both. The flowers are WHITE and very sweet, the leaves are great and thicke, and grow oppositely. It beares a fruite like an APPLE, with fower cavityes in the middle, wherein are seed like those of the Medler, very hard and browne.
The tree is very tender and rare.

THE LAWRELL

In Latine LAURUS REGIA and LAURUS CERASUS. It hath most beautifull large shining greene leaves, and blacke berryes when ripe. It is now well knowne amongst us, and us'd for ornament of North Walles, and within doores for dressing up of potts, and the backes of nosegayes, the great leaves bearing up small flowers against them, and serving for a good shadow to them. The Flowers which are very small and WHITE come forth in May. This tree growes abroad in our gardens, either in standards or against walls and arbours or palissades, and loves a good rich earth. This tree endures the colds of our wynters abroad better than the Bay, and is easily multiplied from slips as well as succours in September and October.

THE HOLLY TREE

Though it is soe common that it growes voluntarily in our woods and hedges, yet being it is a greene that may bee kept with cutting well in any forme, and beautifull both in the leaves and berryes, I have added it to the rest. I have seene a walke of these trees cut into Pyramides, and growing soe very high with leaves from the very ground to the top, that it hath beene a very gratefull sight.

There is a fine variegated kind of Holly, the leaves being stript with yellow and greene, which is all the differences I know of in this tree.

It likes a warme dry soyle, something gravelly, and is hardly transplanted in yong trees to live, but is best encreased from the Berryes.

OF the ARBUTUS

Some call it the STRAWBERRY Tree from the resemblance of its berryes in show to the strawberryes. The leaves are like the Bay but lesse, and of a pleasanter greene, and feel not soe hard. The Flowers are sweet and WHITE, a little like Lilly Convallyes. They come in IULY and AUGUST.

In Ireland there are many of these trees growing wild in the countrey, here in England wee find them very tender, and hardly preserve them with housing in wynter from the Frosts.

Wee encrease them by layers and seed, and esteeme the tree much, as it deserves, both for its beauty and scarcity with us.

OF the ORENGE TREE

In Latine Malus Aurantius. It becomes here in England, with great care and industry, to a tree of two or three yards high. It hath many branches, and growes naturally with a fine round handsome head. The leaves are smooth, pointed at the top but smooth below, of an excellent chearfull greene color, and at the foote of each leafe there is the shape of a little heart, whereon the leafe stands, which distinguishes them from the Lemmon tree. The leaves smell well, but the flowers are deliciously and comfortably sweet, of a pure white color, and consisting of five little leaves. The fruite is well knowne in England, better than the tree, which is only kept in curious gardens by reason of its tendernes.

The Tree flowers with us in June, but in hott countreys hath flowers, leaves, and ripe and greene fruite all the yeare long.

The wild stockes are full of sharpe thornes, but being graffed or enoculated with good kinds, they come no more. Unles the stockes are graffed or enoculated they will not beare till they bee fourteene or fifteene yeares old, but soe in five or six yeares, though we have seldome the fruite come to any good perfection in England, but the curious keepe them only for the sweet flowers, and for the pleasing sight and good sent of their greene leaves. Wee have trees often from Italy and France, but they like not soe well with us, being commonly preiudic'd in the conveyance by sea, as those wee raise here from seed, and graff or enoculate.

The best way to have them live and grow in England is to sow the kernells in the Spring in fine earth, which must bee water'd and kept from the sun when they come up, and being fitt to bee remov'd to bee taken up with the earth about them from the boxes they were sowen in, and sett in gilliflower potts, where they may grow in good sifted earth three or fower yeares, housing them from the end of October till the middle of Aprill. They extreamly delight in sun and moysture, therefore standing abroad in the end of Spring, and all sommer water them plentifully, but in the wynter in the house but seldome, and only in open weather, not in Frosts. The withering of the leaves or shrinking together proceeds as often from want of water and aire as from cold weather, therefore, though they stand in the house, they must not bee long without both. When they grow too bigg for potts, remove them into fresh rich earth, into large wooden cases, about a yard high, narrower at the top than the bottome, made close and joynted like wainscott, with strong iron hookes for two or more to lift them up, & remove them from place to place, and some holes bored through the bottome boards to let passe the water. Plant them in March or Aprill and water them upon planting, and after, but not in frosts. When they have stood long in these vessells take out the old earth, and barbe the rootes, and sett them againe in the same or other vessells fill'd with fresh rich mold, made of fine sifted earth, and very old consum'd dung, and some ashes, if you please, of wood, and bee sure as the trees grow bigg to put them into larger cases every third or fowerth yeare. When any branches are dead, prune them low, & put soft red wax and turpentine mixt with a little rosin on the wounded places to keepe out sun, cold and wett. Give them aire and sometimes water in the house in wynter, in open weather, by setting open the doors and wyndowes of your roome, but take them not forth in to the garden to stand out night and day till the end of Aprill or beginning of May, when all the frosts are past, and let the strong trees stand constantly in the hottest place of ye garden & water them plentifully all sommer.

They have in Italy above twenty severall sorts of Orenges, some sowre, some very sweet, some with a sweetnes and sharpnes mixt together. The best kinds wee know here in England are the China Orenge, a sort lately had from Portugall, whither it came not many yeares since from China. This hath the rind soe pleasant and free from bitternes that it may bee eaten as well as the meate which is sweete, and 'tis the best kind to preserve whole. The SEVILL Orenge, which is of two sorts, sweete & sharpe, and comes from Spaine, and the BERMUDA Orenge which is brought from the Island soe called in the West Indyes, and is the greatest and best, I thinke, of Orenges.

The seed of any of these kinds are excellent to sow, and soe are others of some of the sowrer sorts.

THE LEMMON TREE

In Latine Malum Limonium. The tree is soe like the Orenge tree in flowers and leaves that there is scarce a discernible difference, only this wants the little heart at the foote of the leafe which the Orenge hath, and this tree groweth not soe well in a standard as the other doth, for the branches are weaker, which is the reason that in Italy itselfe they plant it against a wall, but 'tis also true that it needs more heate to ripen the fruite than the Orenge doth.

It flowers when the Orenge doth, and suits with the same government and culture, but it is a little tenderer than the Orenge.

They have in Italy above thirty sorts of Lemmons, but we have very few in England of any kind.

OF THE CITRON TREE

Otherwise called in English the Pomecitron and in Latine MALUM MEDICUM, because it came out of Media, and Malum Citrium. It is very like the Lemmon tree in most things, but the flowers are not soe white, but have a little red mixt with it, and the Fruite is much larger, which wee have often in England, but the tree is rare and tender.

In Italy they have diverse sorts of Citrons, and they call there both Orenge trees, Lemmons, and Citrons by the name of AGRUMI.

OF LAURESTINE

It is a kind of wild Bay, but with lesser and more crumpled leaves. The flowers are WHITE, with a little red at first blowing about the edges, very small and sweet, and grow many together, after which come small blew berryes with a few seeds in them, like the kernells of grapes.

If it stand warme against a wall it beares flowers all the moneths from December to May.

Wee encrease it commonly by layers remov'd in March or Aprill, and kept well water'd. I have not seene the seed sowen, but it must bee the surest way of multiplication, though perhaps the slowest.

OF THE SASSAFRAS TREE

In hot Countreys where it growes naturally, it becomes a great tree, but I have not seen in England any but yong ones of a yeare or two yeares growth, which were rais'd here from seed out of Virginia, and were killed by ye wynters, but I doubt not but they may bee preserved with care, and the tree is worthy of it, for it is very Aromatickely sweet, barke, wood, roote and all, and growes into a very handsome well-headed standard, bearing fine greene leaves like to Sycamores. The wood is called in Latine LIGNUM PAVANUM. More I cannot say but that I heare and read that they are great trees in the West Indyes, and that the wood is physicall.

The PYRACANTHA

Is a kind of ever greene thorne, fittest for hedges, having many sharpe thornes on the boughes. The leaves are of a fine shining greene color, shapt like the Damsons leafe. The Flowers are small, and grow thicke in clusters of a White color with a little eye of blush, after which come berryes like the Hawthornes but more shining.

It flowers in May & June.

This shrubb is very hardy, and is easily encreast by sowing the berryes, and sproutes from the rootes.

OF PHILLYRAEAS

CELASTRUS and ALATERNUS and MACALEB are conceav'd to bee different kinds of Phyllyraeas, but wee are not certaine. Wee have not beene long acquainted with this Greene in England but since wee have knowne it wee have neglected the Pyracantha, and make hedges of this.

Wee have as yet but Three sorts

The PHYLLYRAEA with the broad leafe, which growes very high, and hath fine shining greene leaves growing by paires, somthing like the privett in shape, but of a darker color. The flowers are very small and sweet, and of a yellowish color, which the Bees wonderfully resort to in the end of March and APRILL. This sort is very hardy, enduring ye winters very well, and is best encreast from seed, which wee have now at reasonable rates out of France.

Then there is the PHYLLYRAEA with the narrow leafe, which growes not tall, and is fitt to be kept clipt into little pyramides or Balls or other figures, as the Myrtles are, for ornaments of borders. This is more tender than the former.

Also the PHILLYRAEA with the indented leafe, called usually in Latine Phyllyraea Serrata. The leaves of this are of a sadder greene than the others. It is somwhat tender, and very scarce yet in England.

There is another sort with fine PAINTED or variegated leaves, Yellow or White and greene, which is also tender, and most rare yet with us.

All the kinds have their seed in small blacke Berryes, like Pepper, which wee sow in February and March, and remove the yeare following, yet some old seed will lye a whole yeare in the earth before it comes up.

All the sorts must have a fine rich mold, and a warme place to bee planted in, but the tender sorts wee keepe commonly in tubbs.

ADRACHNE

In English the STRAWBERRY BAY, because the leaves are like the Bay in shape, but not sweetnes. The barke is smooth and shining, red like corall, which cracks and breaks off in Sommer. The Flowers and fruite are like those of the ARBUTUS.

It is tender, and never comes to any considerable bignes with us.

MOLLE

It is a tree brought first into Europe out of PERU in the West

Indyes. It hath a whitish barke, and long smooth branches bending downe towards the earth. The leaves are like Lentills, not notched, hanging on long stalkes, smelling and tasting like pepper. The flowers are very small and white, with reddish chives within, hanging downe in branches of a hand long, and passe into round smooth seed, cover'd with reddish skin, in shape like white pepper.

It flowers in SEPTEMBER.

It is tender, and therefore must have a warme place and good soile. It is encreast by layers, which are long before they take roote.

THE CORALL TREE

Came also out of America, called soe from the color of the flowers, of a fine red. The leaves grow by threes, are in shape and hardnes like the Ivy, and of a pleasant greene color. The boughes have crooked thornes here and there. The seeds are like beanes of a shining red color. It growes easily of the seed, but must bee hous'd in wynter, and well watered in sommer.

OF THE YELLOW JASMYNE of INDIA

Is a low shrub not growing much higher than the Spanish Jasmyn, the Barke is reddish, the branches many, shooting out from the bottome of the stalke. The leaves grow by threes or by fives, are longish, hard like the Pomegranates, thicke, not indented on the edges, of a darke shining greene color. The flowers grow upon the tops of the spriggs, upon such foote stalkes as other Gessamine flowers doe, they have five leaves lesse than those of the Spanish Jasmyn, and blunter at the ends, of a gold yellow colour, and extreame sweet. After the flowers come berryes, as bigg as little olives, with a little seed in them like the kernell of a peare. This sweet Jasmyn is yet rare in England. It is tender, and must bee hous'd in wynter, and well water'd in Sommer, and expos'd to the Hottest Sun. It requires the same culture as the Spanish Jasmyn before mentioned, but hath this in particular to bee lookt to, that no water fall upon the leaves in watering, for they presently grow pale and wither. It is encreast by cutting a twigg to the middle slopewise, putting in a stone (to keepe it open) and covering it with a little sandy earth moistened, and then over that with good earth in a laying pott. Watering it, within a yeare it will take good roote, then take it off from the mother.

It flowers in IULY and AUGUST.

OF MIRTLE

Wee have two sorts of Mirtles, which are soe well knowne I shall not describe them. The leaves and Flowers of both are Very Sweet. That with the NARROW LEAFE, which is of a darke greene color is the MALE, and is fittest to bee clipt into any figure. The other with the BROAD LEAFE of a lighter greene is the FEMALE, whereof there is a Sort which hath very DOWBLE White flowers, wh. are very sweete.

The DOWBLE beareth Flowers most part of the SOMMER, and the other in AUGUST, after which come Berryes.

All these Myrtles are but shrubbs, and soe tender that they seldome endure our wynters abroad, though planted under a south wall yet I have seene some continue soe many yeares. But wee commonly tubb or pott them, and house them carefully as ye tenderest plants.

They love a rich soyle, moysture, and much SUN, and are best encreast by layers, though they will come off slips also, or cuttings.

There is a new sort of Myrtle at Wimbleton, neere London.

OF GALE

In Latine Myrtus Brabantica, because the leaves are somthing like the female Mirtle, but they are longer, thicker and harder, and have a good wholsome sweet aromaticke sent. It is but a low shrubb, and all the branches shoote out from the bottome of the stemme.

The flowers are very small.

This shrub growes abundantly in some moorish grounds in the North parts of England, but is kept in potts by the curious about London, and hous'd in wynter, which it needs not certainly to bee.

IUNIPER

It is a Greene, and strongly resinously sweet, both leaves, wood and berryes. The leaves are small narrow hard and prickly. The bush is but low, and growes plentifully on Chalky hills in the South parts of England, as well as on all barren grounds in hot Countreys.

It hath small Flowers in MAY and the Berryes (like pepper) are ripe in September.

BUTCHERS BROOME or RUSCUS

Is a low shrubb with leaves like those of our common Holly, but lesse, and not soe pricking. The roote is a bunch of great white strings, which spread extreamly in good soyle. It growes wild in Staffordshire & other parts of England, yet is preserv'd in some gardens as a fine greene and a rarity.

BERRY BEARING SAVINE

Is a shrubb very rare with us, but a very fine one. It growes like a Cypres bush, and hath leaves like it, but not soe rough or prickly. In warme countreyes it beares almost continually berryes, like those of Juniper, but few have liv'd with us for long. Wee house it in wynter.

OLEANDER

Hath long narrow light greene smooth leaves, like the OLIVE

tree, but much longer and broader. The BRANCHES shoote out from the roote, soe that this shrubb will not bee kept with a handsome stemme or body. The Flowers are large and tubous, the leaves lying spread open.

Wee have TWO *diversityes of this plant*

One with SCARLET Flowers, which is most common.
Another with WHITE flowers, somwhat rarer.
The RED flowers in July, a little before the White.
These need a good rich earth, and to bee set into vessells to bee transported into the house in wynter, but they cannot endure long without ayre, and therefore must not bee kept soe long close as the other Greenes.
Wee encrease them usually by Layers.

SPANISH BROOME

In Latine Genista Hispanica, and Spartum Hispanicum. It growes up three yards high or more, with long small greene twiggs, and small leaves like ye common broome, and hath YELLOW flowers like it which smell extreamly sweet in hot weather. This kind is reasonable common in our gardens, but that with the WHITE flower is very rare in England.
They flower most part of SOMMER.
These sorts are hardy enough to live abroad with us all wynter, and are easily encreast from the seed, which growes in cods like those of common broome, or succours from the rootes.

SPURGE OLIVE, or MALE LAWRELL

In Latine Laureola mas, or Laureola semper virens, is a very low shrubb with small leaves like a lawrell. The Flowers are greenish, blowing in Autumne and wynter. It is common in England and very hardy and easily encreast from the roote.

WIDOW WAILE

In Latine Chamoelea tricocos, which is one of the kinds, called soe because the berryes grow three together. It is a low shrubb, with many shootes from the roote. The leaves are narrow and dark greene, the flowers pale yellow.
Wee house this shrub in wynter.
The other sort is Chamoelea Alpina, with a greene hoary barke, many slender tough branches, and small roundish leaves, grayish greene above, and hoary underneath. The flowers have but fower leaves, and are of a blush color, after which come small red berryes which turne blacke at length.
This kind is also tender.

SESELI or SESILE AETHIOPICUM

hath many branches sett with leaves like the Willow or Oleander, but lesse much than the last, which smell well. The flowers are small & yellow, and grow in tufts on the tops of the spriggs. The seed is like to Fennell.
It flowreth and seedeth in July and August.
It is a hardy little tree, yet rare with us.

BARBA IOVIS

IUPITERS BEARD, *or the* SILVER BUSH *is a small shrubb.* The barke is hoary, the branches many, the leaves long, whitish hairy and shining, shapt like Lentills, and growing commonly six or seaven together.
The flowers are very small and yellow, growing thicke together on the tops of the branches.
The shrub is rare and tender, and must bee carefully kept from frosts. Wee encrease it from seed.

IUCCA

Like to the Aloes is the Indian Jucca in leafe, and therfore I shall adioyne it here to the Aloes. The stalke growes strong and high,

and beares many flowers hanging downe their heads like the Fritillary or Persian Lilly, but of a faded YELLOW color, with a little tincture of red with it.
It flowers in the Sommer moneths.
It is soe tender that wee must keepe it in tubbs to house it in the wynter. Wee encrease it best from the seed.

Besides these Trees and Shrubbs that are ever greene, wee have some hearbes which keepe their leaves all wynter, and are esteem'd by us for their beauty, such as

MAIDEN HAIRE

In Latine Capillus Veneris, and ADIANTHUM. The French call all the sorts CAPILLAIRES, and value them highly for the variety and lovelines of their greene leaves, for flowers they have no more than the Fearnes have.
One of the best sorts is that of AMERICA described by CORNUTUS, called by writers Adianthum Americanum. It hath many winding purplish branches, besett unevenly, not oppositely with notcht leaves like a cockes combe, of a fine greene colour but spotted with some darker spotts. The roote hath many small darke fibers.
They are to be planted under a North wall, and to continue abroad all wynter. They are encreast by deviding the rootes.

NAVELLWORT

Cotyledon in Latine. The leaves are broad, thicke, fatt and indented, lying on the earth round in a great tuft. The stalke is straight and small, bearing at the top small WHITE flowers with RED spotts on them, of five leaves apiece. The roote is small and thready.
It flowers in the beginning of SOMMER.
There is another lesse sort called the Mountaine Cotyledon.

Here are in the last place added some very Sweet Hearbes, called after the Latine AROMATICKES, *which are yet rare in England*

Ocymum Gentillissimum, a kind of very fine sweet Basill, which is an Annuall. Wee have the seed from Portugall and Spaine.

Marum Syriacum, Assyrian masticke, the leaves are like Marioram and small mirtles. This is tender and hard to raise from seed and very rare here.

Lavendula multifida, Jagged leav'd Lavender, the leaves are whitish and downy, the spike of flowers is bluish like the common Lavender. Sow the seed in Aprill, and house the rootes in Wynter.

Salvia Absynthites, Wormwood Sage. The leafe is like a small sage leafe, but it smells and tasts like wormwood. Bauhinus describes it by the name of Salvia minor altiva.
It is tender and lives not easily abroad all wynter. Encrease it by slips in March or October.

Botrus Chamoedroides. Cut leav'd Germander, and by some Oake of Jerusalem. The leafe is of a sad greene color above, and browne red below. The flowers are very small and grow in clusters like those of the vine. It is an annuall, and scarce, and flowers in August.

Ambrosia sativa, Oake of Cappadocia, it growes two foote high, with many weake crooked streaked branches. The flowers are yellowish and mossy, and all the plant is, as it were, cover'd with a mealy dust. The leaves are deeply cutt like to Muggwort, but thinner and softer. The seed is blacke and round, smelling and tasting well. It is Annuall and flowers in August, & the seed is ripe in September.

Trifolium Odoratum, Sweete Trefoile or Garden Balsame. The stalke growes two cubitts high, shooting out many branches. The leaves grow by threes like other trefoiles. The flowers are small, blew and chaffy. The seed is whitish yellow. The whole is of a whitish greene color. It is sowen in May, flowreth in IUNE and IULY, and the seed is ripe in the end of August.

These following flowers and trees have also a good sent

Beares eares, Woodbinds, Sweet Sultan, Cyclamons of Verona, Persia and the Spring Datura, Maracoc, Geranium triste, Stockes, Wallflowers, Orientall hyacinths, The Tuberous Hyacinth, Spanish Jasmyn, Yellow Indian Jasmyn, Common white Jasmyn, many Bulbous Irises, Jounquilles, Lilly Convally, White Lilly, yellow Lilly, Asphodell, Saponaria, White Syringa, Persian Jasmyn, Wonder of Peru, Mezereum Germanicum, Muscari, Violetts, Cowslips, Primroses, Daffodills, Nasturtium Indicum, Mountaine Nard, Gilliflowers, Pinkes, Pansyes, Orenge flowers, yellow Portugall Ranuncules, Apples of Paradise, Roses, Hesperis Saffran, Mirtles, Laurustine flowers, Sweet olive, and Spanish broom flowers.

Here are also added Remembrances of what is to bee done in a GARDEN every Moneth of the Yeare, and what plants are usually in FLOWER in each Moneth in England

JANUARY

These only Beare flowers this cold Moneth: viz. WYNTER ACONITE, BLACKE HELLEBORE, WYNTER CYCLAMENS, PRIMEROSES, Clusius his first IRIS, and somtimes the PERSIAN IRIS, LAURUSTINE.

Remembrances for this Moneth

Cover such plantes as are anything tender and stand abroad against hard Frosts, as also SEEDES sowen in potts and cases, but give them ayre in open weather.

Sett potted Anemones and Beares eares and Cyclamens and other weake rootes out of violent raines and Snowes, as also potts and cases of Seedes, or else bow the potts downe on the earth in such weather, that they may not receave too much wett at a tyme, nor the earth bee washt away.

Baite trapps for garden Mice and Moles with Kernells of Nutts, Walnutts, Almonds, or Chestnutts.

FEBRUARY

The same that flower in January flower also this Moneth, and soe doe all sorts of CROCUSSES, SINGLE HEPATICAES, the SINGLE thin-leav'd ANEMONES, and some PLUSH ANEMONES that stand very warme, and were sett in the beginning of Wynter or end of Autumne, some POLYANTHES DAFFODILLS, the BULBOUS VIOLET, the MEZEREON TREE.

Remembrances for this Moneth

In the beginning of this Moneth observe the directions of January. In the middle and end of this moneth sow on hot bedds tender plants, and such as flower soe late that they otherwise would not perfect their seed with us before the approach of wynter, such as AMARANTHES, INDIAN CANES, MARACOCS, DATURAES, APPLES of LOVE, and of ETHIOPIA, BALSAMINAES and the like, preserving them well with covers and glasses when they come up.

In the end of this Moneth put fresh sifted mold to the rootes of Beares eares, Tulipes, Anemones, Hepaticaes, and other choice flowers, upon the olde earth, not stirring the rootes, but to cherish and defend the plants against the March wyndes. This will make them come on and prosper very much.

MARCH

PRIMROSES, COWSLIPS, violetts, white CROCUSSES, single and DOWBLE HEPATICAES, the EARLY small STAR HYACINTHES, ALL the ORIENTALL HYACINTHES, DENS CANINUS, ALL SORTS OF ANEMONES, single and DOWBLE, if sett betimes, DWARFE flagg IRISES of severall colours, Little dowble PILEWORT, ALL SORTS almost of NARCISSI, SOME EARLY TULIPES, ALL SORTS of BEARES EARES, SPRING CYCLAMENS, FRITILLARYES, WALLFLOWERS, Stocke Gilliflowers, Leucoium Hexaphyllon, Leucoium Tryphyllon, Lauristine, Mezereon.

Remembrances for this Moneth

In the beginning put fresh fine mold to Tulipes, Anemones and Beares eares, and other forward flowers. Uncover plants in faire dayes, and cover them againe before night, and in wyndy or stormy weather. Cover choice Tulipes in frosty nights, for many are killed in this moneth by the frosts & wyndes, the harme appeares first by the white spotts on the leaves.

Digg up gravell walkes, and cleanse your ground, & lay it neate.

Lay layers of all fine trees and Shrubbs.

Plant BOX for compartments.

Transplant Spanish Jasmyns, Orenge trees, Myrtles, Oleanders, Pomegranates, and such tender trees (but better in August).

Transplant Autumnall cyclamens, and other autumnall plants.

Plant all manner of Fibrous plantes that are not this moneth in flower.
Plant the Tuberous Hyacinths in potts.
Sow Gilliflower seed, Stockes, Scarlet Beane, Wonder of Peru, Indian Pepper, Sour Apples, Maracocs, and such tender seeds as are mentioned the last moneth on hott beds, the rest in good earth.
In the end of this moneth take out Myrtles, Oleanders, and the hardiest Greenes and Gilliflowers out of the wynter house, and sett them abroad in the shade ten dayes or a fortnight, to inure them to the ayre before you bring them into hott sun, which otherwise will hurt them.
Water a little in the end of this moneth in warme dayes, about noone or before, & not neare night.

APRILL

Primroses, Cowslips, Violetts, Beares eares, All Sorts of Dowble and single Anemones, All manner of Tulipes, Fritillaryes, Muscaries, Dwarfe flagg Irises, Diverse sorts of Daffodills, all sorts of Jounquilles, Late orientall hyacinthes, English Hyacinthes, Starr Hyacinthes, Grape Hyacinthes, feather'd or hairy Hyacinthes, Spring cyclamons, Crowne Imperiall, Dogtooth violett, single and dowble Stockes, Dowble Hepaticaes, Asian Ranuncules, Pulsatillaes, Daysies, Iris of Florence, Sena Scorpiodes, Arbor Judae, Persian Jasmyn, Woodbynd.

Remembrances for APRILL

Divide and sett all manner of Fibrous plants, which are not in flower, or were not the last moneth.
Sow seeds of all sorts of Annualls in the plaine earth, without hott beds, but not too much in the sun.
Transplant Autumnall cyclamens, and other autumnalls.
Take forth of your wynter house all Greenes and other things remaining there.

Cover fine tulipes and other choice flowers from the violent heate of the sun, and hayles and stormes.
If the weather be dry, water well potts and cases, and Anemones and Ranuncules in the earth.

MAY

Some late Tulipes, some single and dowble white Narcissi, Narcissus tertius Matthioli, the great late Bulbous Violet, Hayry Hyacinthes, Starr Hyacinthes of Peru, other sommer starr hyacinthes, Ornithogalum Arabicum, Ornithogalum Neapolitanum, other Ornithogalums, Phalangium Allobrogicum, other Phalangiums, the Chalcedonian Iris, other flagg Irises, the great blew bulbous Iris, Cyani, Caltha palustris, Cotyledons, Gladioli, Stockes, Foxgloves, severall sorts of Satyriums and Orchises, Moathmulleins, Geraniums, yellow Martagon lillyes, yellow Asphodell, Orenge early Lilly, Lichnises, Daisyes, White and yellow Molyes, Pansyes, Anemones planted in the Spring, Ranuncules, (Queene May, alias the dowble white Ranuncule), the early red Martagon, Sedum Serratum, Dowble Sysimbrium, Valerians, Muske Gilliflowers, Peonyes, Persian Lilly, some wynter podds of Gilliflowers, All manner of Roses (but the muske Rose), at the end of the moneth Laburnum, Cytisus, Colutaea, Acacia, Lilacs (white and blew), Syringa, Fraxinella, Woodbind, Persian Jasmyn.

Remembrances for May

Transplant Autumnall cyclamens.
Devide Hesperis rootes.
Gather Anemone seed in sunshine, and sow it presently as you will.
Sow Annuall's seed.
Cover tulipes from sun.
Gather Iris stalkes, and sticke them in moist earth in the house to keepe long fresh.

Satyriums, Pansyes, Thlaspi, the great white spiked Ornithogalum, some wynter podds of Gilliflowers, all the sorts of Gladioli, most Lillyes, the Imperiall, the white, the yellow and Pomponium Martagon, and that of Canada, Nasturtium Indicum, Lychnises, All sorts of bulbous Irises (except the Persian and prima Clusii), Bellflowers, Valerians, white and red, the Indian Tuberous white Hyacinth, Double Featherfew, Dowble Ptarmica, Dowble stockes, Convolvuli, Venus looking glasse, Larkeheeles, Snapdragons, Cyani, Foxgloves, Geraniums, Stockes, Spiderworts of Virginia, Spanish broome, Fraxinella, the red and the white, Clematis pannonica, Woodbinds, Syringa, White and Yellow Jasmyns, Sweet Olive, Orenge trees, Goates rue, Roses of all sorts except the muske rose, and the Cinnamon, which is past before the end of this moneth.

Remembrances for June

Sow Annuall seeds for to flower in Autumne.
Gather the seeds of Hyacinthes, Narcissi, Beares eares and Ranuncules, and sow them presently if you please.
Take up Anemones and Ranuncule rootes.
Take up Tulipes, if well wither'd.
Enoculate Jasmyns, Roses and other shrubbs.
In the end of this moneth begin to take up naked rootes, and Spring cyclamens, Muscaryes, Martagons, Crownes Imperiall, Fritillaryes, and the like which will not keepe long out of the ground, and plant them againe as soon as may bee.

IULY

Dowble Ptarmica and Featherfew, All sorts of Gillyflowers, White and red Lillyes, the Orenge spotted Martagon, Convolvuli, Scabious, Amaranthes of severall colours, White and blew bellflowers, Sweet Sultan, Acanthus or Brane Ursine, Anagalis Lusitanica, Indian Canes, Cyclamens of Verona and the sweet purple, Datura, Elychrison, Geranium triste and of Crete, Yellow Wallflowers, the Tuberous Hyacinth, Limonium, white dowble Lychnis, Wonder of Peru, Nasturtium Indicum, French Marigolds or Africans, Larkesheeles, yellow Pansy, Maracoc, Scarlet beane, Thlaspi of Crete, most Annualls, Hollyhockes.

In the beginning of the moneth severall Roses, Woodbinds, Fraxinellas, Oleanders, severall Clematises, Dowble and single Pomegranate, Spanish Jasmyn, sweet yellow Jasmyn, Mirtles, Orenge trees, Muske rose.

Remembrances for Iuly

Cut box in borders.

Take up Spring Cyclamens, and such rootes as were directed to bee taken up the last moneth, and to bee quickly replanted.

Take up such Tulipes as were left in the earth, and Anemones and all bulbous rootes not taken up before.

Gather and sow the seed of Spring cyclamens in potts.

Sow Anemone seed.

Lay layers of Gilliflowers.

Graft and enoculate Mirtles, Orenges, Jasmyns, Roses and other fine shrubbs.

AUGUST

Almost all that flower'd the last moneth are also in flower this moneth, and Aster Atticus, or the Blew Marigold.

Remembrances for this moneth

Sow Anemone seed, covering it lightly, setting it in the shade, and watering it often with a fine pot.

Sow Narcissus seed, and orientall jacynths.

Lay layers of Gilliflowers.

Plant single anemones of each kinde, to have flowers in Autumne and in the Spring betimes.

Autumnall Cyclamens, some Beares eares, Colchicums, Aster Atticus, Snapdragons, Violetts, Indian Canes, great dowble Daysies, Flower of the sun, White bells, Geraniums, the Annuall Gentianella, Tuberous Hyacinth, Lychnises, Limoniums, Indian Narcissi, Marvel of Peru, Nasturtium Indicum, Persian Narcissus, Africans, Amaranthes, Pansyes, Apples of Aethiopia, Thomy apples, Indian Peppers, Datura, Maracoc, Spiderworts of Virginia, Scarlet Beane, Great Mouseare, Portugall Ranuncules (dowble and single), Purple Volubilis, Thlaspi, Amomum Plinyi, Laurustinus in the end of the moneth, Spanish Jasmyn, sweet Indian Jasmyn, Orenge trees, Balaustium, Althaea frutex, Myrtles, Clematis, Monethly Rose, and Muske Rose.

Remembrances for September

Plant all sorts of Anemones and Ranuncules.
Slip gilliflowers and stockes.
Remove all Greenes.
Devide or remove Beares eares, and all other Fibrous perenniall plants if you please.
Sow seed of Beares eares, Ranuncules, Irises, Martagons, Crowne Imperialls, Lillyes, Tulipes, & other bulbous plants.
Sow Annuall seeds that are strong and not subject to frosts, such as Larkes Spurrs, Nigella, Scabious, &c, to flower betimes in Sommer & bring good seed.
Remove dowble Hepaticaes.

OCTOBER

Most which flower in September flower also this moneth, and Saponaria also, and some Primroses.

Remembrances for October

Plant, sow, devide and remove all mentioned in September to bee done soe to.

In the end of the Moneth howse the tenderest plants and shrubbs, giving them ayre enough through wyndowes and doores.

NOVEMBER

Snapdragons, Stockes, Daysies, many single Anemones, and some dowble, Wynter Persian cyclamen, Blacke Ellebore, Laurustyne.

Remembrances for November

Plant Anemones, Roses, Althaea frutex, Lilacs, Syringaes, Cytisi, and generally all shrubbs that loose their Leaves in Wynter, and such as are not very ill able to endure frosts, wh. must bee planted in September or October.
Plant Peonyes, tuberous Irises, and such strong rootes.
Plant and sow fibrous plants and seedes spoken of in September.
Plant your choicest Tulipes.
Prepare coverings for your tender plants abroad.

DECEMBER

Wynter Cyclamen, the common and the Persian, Iris prima Clusii, Blacke Hellebore, some single Anemones that stand warme, Laurustine.

Remembrances for December

Cover your tender plants in Frosts, and observe all the directions for January.
Lay earth and dung on heapes to rott and make molds.
Make a little fire in your wynter house for Greenes on frosty nights.

OF WALL FRUITE

CHERRYES Fruite trees proper for ordinary WALLS under 9 foote high, are the MAY CHERRY, the DUKE CHERRY, (but the walls must bee higher for the following) WHITE, BLACKE, and RED HEARTS, the Blacke is best, the Caroone Cherry, the Orleans cherry (a new cherry), and they are to be sett against West or East Walls.

PLUMS The CHERRY PLUM, alias the Queene Mother PLUM, the DAMAZEENE, the CHESTON PLUM, the PERDIGAN, the AMBER plum, the MOROCCO plum, the MARBLES PLUM, the MUSCLE PLUM, the great Holland plum (a new plum), Monsieur's plum, Altisse plum, Mirabelle, Pigeon's Heart plum, White Damas. plum. The North and West Walls will serve for PLUMMS, but the East or South are much better.

PEACHES All very good The Red and WHITE NUTMEG PEACH, very early & small, The NEWINGTON, the Admirable Peach, The Primordian peach, the BELLOWES PEACH, the SAVOY PEACH, the PAU Peach, the PERSIAN, the RAMBOUILLAN Peach, the MODENA, the Orleans, the Superintendent, the Smyrna, the La Varre, the Sion Peach, the Admirable, the Lawrente, the Magdalen. PEACHES must bee set against East or South Walls.

APRICOCKES The GREAT APRICOCKE, the MASCULINE Early Apricocke, The ORENGE APRICOCKE, FRUITE de NOVO. Apricockes need a high wall, and to stand against South or East walls, shelter'd from Wind and much RAINE.

CORNELIAN I know but one sort of CORNELIAN, which is the

red, and that will run up high, and needs an East or South wall.

NECTORAN The RED ROMAN NECTORAN, the MURREY Nectoran, the GREENE NECTORAN, the Elrug or Gurle's Nectoran (which comes from a stone, and is rare yet, 1661) also the ESSEX nectoran, and the WHITE nectoran, both wh. come from the stone.

Nectorans must have a South or East wall.

PEARES PEARES for WALLS are only us'd to bee with us the WINTER BON CHRESTIEN, and the WYNTER BERGOMOTS, the other sorts bearing well enough in Standards.

The first runs very high, and is therefore set against high houses, or walls of 14 or 15 foote high (and therefore should be grafted on quince stockes). The other growes lower. East or South high walls for these peares, other aspects may grow other peares. [Monsieur John and the Beurre pears are all good Wynter pears.]

VINES VINES may bee kept low under 10 foote, and may bee suffer'd well to run high. The sorts fittest for England are the PARSLEY VINE, the WHITE MUSCADINE, the RED FRONTINIAC, and the YELLOW FRONTINIAC.

[The D'Arbois vine, white grape, very good, the Muscat, the Auvergne.]

Vines must stand against an East or South wall.

APPLES APPLES are seldome planted against walls, yet some set the Maudlin apple, a good sommer apple, and the Janetting against walls to make the fruite well coloured.

All Fruite against walls must bee grafted or enoculated very low.

FRUITE TREES for HEDGES or PALISSADES,
under 10 foote high commonly

CODLING APPLES, PEAREMAINS, any SOMMER APPLES.

SOMMER BERGAMOT PEARES, Sommer BON CHRESTIEN PEARES, SLIP PEARES, and almost all other sorts of PEARES.

DUKES, FLANDERS, and CARNATION CHERRYES.

ALL SORTS of PLUMMS.

ALL SORTS of QUINCES.

VINES of all sorts.

The manner of making the hedges is either with streight poles set upright with others acrosse, about a foote or two asunder, bound together, or with tymber and crosse rayles. Some make the Fruite trees to spreade their boughes by cutting them, and to grow without helpe of rayles or poles.

Some plant the Hedges all of one sort of Fruite together, others mix severall sorts, but the CHERRYES and PEARES and VINES should have most of the sun.

These Hedges they set about great square Quarters in large Gardens in France.

Fruite against Palissades or Hedges must bee grafted very low.

FRUITE TREES for an ORCHARD or STANDARDS

APPLES *Wee have many sorts of* APPLES, some of the *Sommer* season, such as DOVE BILLS, CODLINGS, Janettings, many of *Autumne* as Queenings, Darlings, Golden Pippens, and many sorts of *Wynter* as Pippens and Pearemaines. Apples blossome not here till the last week of Aprill, and first weeke of May, but where the ground is rich, & the trees stand warme, & sheltered, they blossome at least ten dayes sooner.

Some keepe almost the whole yeare about, such as PIPPENS, APPLEJOHNS or DEUXANS, some RUSSETTINGS, & one kinde of pearmaine.

The apples called in France De Manerbe, and Hautbois have always a very faire high stem, & forme a handsome head, with tall and straight boughs, soe that loaden carts may goe under them. Their fruite is not subject to fall, & excellent for Sider.

APPLES beare well only in a rich CLAY, or MARLE SOYLE, or a very rich deepe gravelly soyle.

PEARES *Wee have also many sorts of* PEARES fitt for Standards. Some EARLY, such as the KATHERINE PEARE.

Some middle season'd such as the SOMMER BERGAMOT, the SOMMER BON CHRESTIEN, the NORWICH, the WINSORE, the SLIP PEARE, the BINFIELD or Dove Peare, Messire John, Roy d'esté, the LEWYS peare, St Michel's peare, St Lesin peare, the Beurré peare, the long greene peare.

Some of the end of Wynter, as the FINOR (a French peare), the SPANISH WARDEN, the BISHOPS PEARE, the Dowble flower'd peare, the Wynter thorne peare.

PEARES prosper and beare best in a rich gravelly, or somwhat sandy mold, but not too barren a sand.

Some peares blossome in the end of March, the rest in Aprill, I meane if standards. The late wynter peares, such as the Spanish Warden, & others, blossome with the first.

PLUMMS *Wee have many sorts of* Plums for standards, some few blossome in the end of March, but most in the beginning or middle of Aprill, before Cherryes or Apples, but a little after some early peares. The Marbled Plum, and the Turkey plum are ripe in the end of July at the furthest, against a wall.

The Muscle plumm was ripe in standards with mee the beginning of August.

Plums for walls. The Great Holland plum, a new great

white plum, the Turkey plum, the Catalonia plum, the Cheston plum, the Orleans plum, alias Lambert's plum, very good, the Lord Says plum, excellent good, the little round greene plum, very sweet & good, the Matchles plum, very good, the Marbled plum, good, the Muscle plum, good, and the white perdigan Plums prosper best in a light loose soyle, indifferent rich. They love to bee shelter'd from cold wynds.

CHERRYES Only the Flanders and the Carnation cherry doe well in England in standards. White Hearts, if they stand warme, and the Gascoyne Cherry will beare indifferent well also in Standards, and the [Red] if they are well sheltered from winds.

The best Cherryes for walls are the Duke, the Blacke Heart, a new cherry, the Red Heart, a good sort, the White Heart, the Caroone cherry, the Orleans cherry, a new sort, and the Carnation late cherry, which beares ill in Standards unless well shelter'd from wynds.

Cherryes love a light sandy earth or loame, & to stand warme, and shelter'd.

The earlier sorts blossome in the middle of Aprill, the other sorts in the end of Aprill, the Carnations last.

QUINCES *Wee have* the Portugall Quince which is the best, and the small round Quince.

They thrive better in standards than against a wall, and love a rich moist earth, and to bee often overflowed with water, or to have sinkes or other waters run over the earth where they grow, but the water must not stay too long on.

They must not bee expos'd to sharp wynds.

Quinces blossome in the end of Aprill.

MEDLARS Medlars blossome in Aprill. . . .

The Vine prospers not in a wett soyle, nor in a stiffe clay, nor other strong earth. The best earth is a sandy, or loose earth, though also they beare curious wyne in a stony or rocky earth. In a very rich blacke soyle they yield a course rough wyne, soe that the best is a sandy earth, helpt often with ashes or rotten old dung, as shall bee said hereafter.

The best situation of a Vine is against the East or South east sun, or the South; the West is the worst except the North. The vines must stande warme, shelter'd with hills or walls or some fences from the Northerne or Westerne winds.

Vines may bee multiplyed easily by laying downe branches as they grow to the olde roote or stocke, in little trenches of about a foote deepe, and covering the branches with fine mold, letting not above two rowes (or three at most) of eyes or buds come out of the earth. It is best that the branches you lay downe bee at least of two yeares shott wood, & not of the last yeare's shoots, at leaste soe much of the branch as is cover'd and lay'd in the earth, if that which comes forth bee new wood, it matters not soe much. It is said by an Italian writer that if a branch like a graft of one vine, be piec'd to another, by cutting the ends of each branch aslant to the heart, & tying them close together, and laying them cover'd in the earth as aforesaid, they will take.

Vines may bee lay'd either in Autumne, Wynter or Spring at any tyme except in Frosts, not regarding the moone. I thinke the Autumne best. If they sproute forth as they lye, doe not prune them, nor cut them.

Vines are also multiplyed by succours taken from rootes of vines, and by cuttings of vine branches. The cuttings are of two sorts, either cuttings only of the new wood, that is of the last yeare's shootes, or of the new wood with a little of the olde wood at the foote thereof, like a clubb or hammer head, which the Italians call Tagliolo a Martello, and Zocca.

The best tyme to sett these cuttings is betymes in the Spring, viz. February in the wane of the moone, if the frosts permitt, March is next best, then Aprill before they bud. In three yeares cuttings will beare in Italy.

Plant your cuttings of vines in your vineyard in a direct line within two or three feete of each other, but let the rowes bee on levell ground fower or five feete distant from one another, that the vines shadow not each other.

The ground must bee digg'd well thus before you plant yr cuttings. First make a square plott with paths about it, and lesser walkes through it, either acrosse or otherwise. Then digge a deepe ditch of three foote deepe, and as many foote broad, throwing that earth upon the outside, and then digge another such ditch as neare the former as may bee, throwing the earth which comes out of the second ditch into the first, & soe another ditch till your square bee finish'd, and let this bee done a moneth or two or more before you plant your vines, that the earth may bee light. Then when you plant make a hole with a bigg stake of wood, & put in it either dust of [?] or very old mucke turn'd to earth, having first planted your cutting in it, two foote deepe or more. This square for cuttings is called Lo Scassato.

If you will plant a ground with rooted vines, you neede make ditches or holes of a yarde broad, and as much deepe. Make these holes in August, if you plant yr rootes before wynter, as in September or October; and in December if that you plant them not till the Spring, as in February or March.

When you plant these rootes first, if there bee any small stones in your ground, throw them into the bottome of your ditch, then throw some earth on them, then place your plants about three feete asunder from each other, and two rowes in a ditch. You may also plant a club cutting with olde wood betwixt every roote, for somtimes they take better than the rootes.

Spread your rootes every way handsomely on the earth, and

then cover them with some fine rich mold or dust, and then old rotten dung over that, or leaves or small twiggs of vines, or other such things if you please, to keepe the earth light. Then fill up the ditch with earth almost full, but not altogether, that moysture may come to the rootes till Aprill bee past, & then fill them up high, that the earth may defend the rootes from the hot sun.

Plant your cuttings slopewise in the ground that they may roote the better, & let all sorts of cuttings or rootes to plant have only two or three budds at most above the ground.

If your cuttings bee not new cutt when you plant them, you must cutt of a little of the lower end, and bee sure to take your cuttings of such places of the stockes as have borne grapes that yeare, & cut them not till afternoone, and in the encrease of the moone, & from that side in vineyards next the South or South-east.

Veca Angela, Chiocca, and Montonego will keepe best of any vines in the wynter.

They use to beare up the vines in Italy first with canes or reedes, the second yeare with chestnutt stakes, and then with willowes, or olives which corrupt not, or chestnutts, *Ottimi di rovere spaccata.*

You neede not digg the earth the first yeare after it is planted, but hoe away the yong grasse or weeds, but all other yeares afterwards you may digge the earth more or lesse at any tyme but when the vines are in flower, or when the earth is wett.

Digg deepe an olde vineyard & take away, and if you thinke the earth too barren by reason of the poornes of the shootes or by other signes, then mend it with ashes or dust or very olde dung of cowes, or espetially pigeons dung, well rotted, applyed in November, but let not the dungs touch the rootes, but lye neere them upon the earth.

The pruning of vines well is of greatest difficulty, and cannot have rules given soe well for it, but that there needs an experienced pruner to doe it.

Generally seeke in vineyards to keepe the stockes or bodyes of your vines not above two foote high or thereabouts. Leave upon this head one cheife or master branch (they call it in Italian tralce or catena or Capomaestro) let this master branch bee left halfe a yard or a yard long, according to the strength of the vine, and let it bee the principall amongst the branches, and of the last yeares shoote, and the lowest of the other branches must bee pruned very low or short, leaving only one eye or budd, or two at the most, and this short branch (which the Italians call sperone, or sedone or segone) is to serve to send forth a master branch for the next yeare, cutting of the other master branch which was left the last yeare. This vine being thus prun'd, cut away all the rest of the other branches except those two aforesaid, except you judge the vine soe vigorous that it can nourish dowble as much.

Then prune away all the shootes neere the ground or under the earth, unles you meane to take away the olde roote, & supply it with a new shoote (these shootes are called Capparelli and Caprioti).

Note that when you cut the vine weeping it weepe not upon the eye or bud, and cut the branch obliquely or aslant, and not round, that it may weepe the better.

The tyme of pruning vines is from the end of February till the end of March, in the decrease of the moone, they who have many beginn somwhat sooner.

The master branch must bee tyed to a stake, bending downe its head archwise towards the earth, for if the heads stand upright the nourishment will stop at the first buds, & the Pampini would grow from thence only strong, but those from the buds above would bee weake & small, and beare fewer grapes for want of nourishment.

Every yeare the vines must be prun'd anew, and tyed and digged, the oftner digged the better.

Too much mucke makes a vine shoote out much wood, but beare few grapes.

After a plentiful vintage prune low, & if the vines bee ill prune close, and nourish a succor from the roote instead of the mother. Never tye the vines twice in ye same place of the branch, & tye not higher than two eyes in the new shootes.
In Italy only La Lugliatica or Tremorina grow against houses or Pergole, as of a nature to grow high & require sun. They eate those, and make not wyne of them. Fat earth makes them Morbide. If you would have them or other vines to growe high, plucke of the lower eyes of the branches.
The youth of vines is the first yeares, the virility till they bee ten yeares olde, & their olde age till twenty. In their youth prune them close or low to get them a stocke or a bodye, and in their old age also to maintaine them in vigor.

My owne observations of Vines

Plant good strong cuttings of the same yeares shootes in February, or at furthest in the beginning of March, let the cuttings bee of fower eyes in length, & thrust two of the rowes of eyes wholy into the ground, and let the other two stand a little slope out of the earth. These cuttings will put forth leaves at the eyes in the beginning of May, if they bee set in good earth, and in somwhat a shady place, but some little sun doth not harme them. They will bee rooted well enough to remove in a yeares tyme, or in the second yeare at the most. Let the cuttings bee set in the earth with the eyes or knots upwards as they grow.
Few cuttings will misse taking thus, also cuttings may bee a moneth or more out of the earth and grow, soe they bee not kept too hott to dry very much.
Water your cuttings in dry earth and dry weather often.
The newer your cuttings are sett, that is the sooner after they are cutt from the tree, the better to take roote.
Remove rooted vines in March or the end of February.
[Prune] your vines, lest they bleed, in the end of February.
Vines that beare white grapes have a darker greene leafe at the

beginning than the blew or blacke grape vines, and the white grape vines leaves are a little reddish or brownish at the first coming forth.

Vines beginn here in Wales to bud in the beginning, & to put out their leaves in the end of Aprill.

The best kinds of vines wee have in England are:

The common white Muscadine, it beares and likes well with us, and ripens very well.

The early white Muscadine, with large grapes.

The ordinary Frontiniacke, it ripens not well here.

The Red Frontiniacke.

The blood red Grape, very ripe and sweet here, as Sir J. W. assures me.

The curran grape, a very small grape.

The Parsley grape, a white grape, it beares very much, and ripens reasonable well; it is called the parsley grape because the leaves are more iagged and deeper cutt than those of other vines.

The soyle of this vineyard (which was a part of Blackheath, neere Greenwich in Kent) is extreame barren (as it seemes to bee) of a light whitish sand, mixt with small stones. On the earth naturally growes nothing but ling and furze.
The situation is on the side of a hill, which lyes full facing on the south, well defended by the hills from the north and west wynds.
The parcell of ground was betwixt one & two acres.
The earth was in the sommer tyme or autumne digged into shallow trenches or ridges.
A little before or after Christmas, as the weather was open and faire, the yong rooted vines (which came most from cuttings, and were of three yeares growth before removell hither) were set in the trenches in straight lines, a yarde asunder each vine.
Betwixt each ranke of vines there was a path of 4 foote wide to goe betwixt the vines, & digg & prune them. From each roote two of ye strongest shootes only were suffer'd to grow up every yeare, which were tyed up to a stake of about 4 feete high, and soe stood till the tyme vines beginn to sprout out (wh. was in Aprill) and then the tops of each of these two shootes are bound downe to a stake, stucke betwixt every two rootes, & tyed archwise to the said stake, one of the two branches is tyed to the right hand stake & the other to the left hand stake.
These two shootes aforesaid bowed soe downe, put forth yong branches at the ioynts, which will fall and hang downe to the very earth, and beare grapes to the ground. The lowest grapes are sweetest, and are ripe soonest because of the reflexion from the earth.
Every yeare the roote from whence the aforesaid two shootes grew will put forth severall new shootes, which must bee suffer'd all to grow till pruning tyme, which is from Christmas till March.
In that tyme you must cut away the said two olde shootes within

one ioynt of the head of the olde stocke (which head should not bee a foote higher than the earth), and suffer the two strongest shootes of this last yeare to stand up, to bee tyed to the stake till they are arched over in Aprill or March as aforesaid. Then you must cutt away all the sproutes and shootes besides these two, except two only which must bee the strongest next to the first two, and these two must not bee cutt of neerer than two eyes or ioynts of the stocke, & are left soe to serve for the two shootes for the yeare following, when the other two shootes are cutt away, & this order must bee us'd yearly in the pruning of these vineyard vines. The pruning of vines wh. grow high on walls or trees is quite another way.

Colonell Blunt says that vines cannot stand too dry, nor never need watering, and prosper best in a shallow earth, where the rootes cannot run downe deepe, as on rockes or gravell.

Springs must bee drained away from a vineyard, if there bee any; the rootes cannot endure wett.

The Colonell sayth hee uses no dung nor compost to this barren earth of his vineyard, which is very strange.

The ground must bee kept clean'd from weeds, with howeing, and the weeds may lye to rott about the rootes.

The fittest vines for a vineyard in England are thought to bee the White and the Red Muscadine, the red corant grape with stones, & the small frontiniacke vines, as good as any or better.

VINES

The white grape from my Lord Peters is a very good sweete grape, & bore well 1669, was ripe that yeare in the middle of September.

The red Wimbleton grape in the Court beares very thicke, and is *very good*, but not ripe till the end of Sept. 1669.

Muscat de Frontignan very good. I had it from Orleans.

Early Auvergne, I had it with the former from Orleans.

The Darbois vine. A white grape, very good.

The true Raisin of the Sun Vine beares a great long red grape.

The Lombardy vine, as Rose calls it, the King's gardiner, beares a faire red grape wh. the King loves.

The Rhenish vine beares a white longish grape, very good, but must have a very warme wall.

The Blew or Red Frontiniacke, a round red grape, not very bigg, but very sweete and musky, requires a good hot sun.

The Cluster Currans vine, the bunches close set with small blew grapes, very sweete and good & great bearers.

Diverse sorts of Muscat grapes wh. are tender & need very warme walls.

A list of Fruite trees & flowers with the prices, sent mee from George Ricketts, of Hogsden, London. November, 1667

Peaches and Nectorans

The Murrey Nectoran	3 sh.
Red Roman Nectoran	3 sh.
Tawney Nectoran	3 sh.
Painted Nectoran	3 sh.
White Nutmeg Peach	2 sh.

Newingtons, 2 sorts
Bellowes Peach
Morillion Peach
Peach de Pau
Rambouillon Peach
Portugall
Carnation
Savoy
Orleans
Red Nutmegg
Roman
Queenes Peach
Withy Peach
Royall
Muske
Arabian Peach

All these peaches above without prices sett to them are at 2 shill. the tree.

Cherryes

Dukes
Flanders
Mayes

Morillions
Red
White } Hearts
Blacke
Amber
Prince Royall
Carnation

All these cherryes at 8d. the tree.

Peares

Winter Bon Chrestien
Somer Bon Chrestien
Wynter Muske
Sommer Muske
Bergamot de Bugi
Wynter Bergamot
Somer Bergamot
Wynter Wyndsor
Somer Wyndsor
Beurré de Roy
Flower Peare
Norwich peare
Rosewater peare
Bellamus peare
Mounsieur John
Painted peare
Ladyes Buttocke
Geniting peare
Thatcher
White Robin
Moleborne
Greenfield
Dove Peare

Lewys Peare
Bishops Fencer
Spanish Warden
English Warden
Norwich Warden
Blacke peare of Worcester
White Worcester
Russet Katherine
Pound peare
Orenge peare
Pettworth peare

All these peares are at 12d. the tree.

Apples

Sommer Pepin
Holland Pepin
Russet pepin
Kentish pepin, the best suppos'd in England
Russetings
Gilliflowers
Muscadine Queene, a good somer fruite
King Apple
John Apple
Golden Rennetts
Royall pearemains
Hollow-crown'd pearemains
the Common Pearemaine
Great Apple of England
Figg apple without a core
Nonsuch apple
Old wife

All these apples are at 8d. the tree, except the Figg apple wh. is 5 shillings.

July flowers

Oylman, purple & white
Leckerbett, cr. & wh.
Virgin of Middlesex
Empire of Dalfast
Bride of Holland. sc. & wh.
Dutches of Yorke
Empire of Russia
Coridon. cr. & wh.
Emperours Court c. & w.
Princes Court. c. & w.
Marble Stone. p. & w.
Cocke. s. & w.
Chancelor
Crowne of Bohemia
King of Assyria p. & w.
Purple Paragon
Yong Prince s. & w.
Virgin of England
House of Commons p. & w.
Belle Infanta c. & w.
Tamberlaine c. & w.
Generall of Holland
Queene Catherine c. & w.

All these Gilliflowers are at 18d. the roote, one with another.
Nov. 1667.

My peares

Monsieur is a brown round peare like to the common Bergamot.

The King peare soe called by Rose because the King liked it, but it is a French peare, I know not the name, it is a browne, round, moyst, musky peare, ripe with mee in Sept. very good, good bearer in standards.

The Thorne peare, a greene longish peare, but small this first yeare of its bearing, being 1677.

Spanish Bon Chretien, a long faire browne and red peare, this yeare 1677.

Wynter Beurre, a long light greene peare, not large this first yeare of its bearing, being 1677.

Anemones bought of Le pere, Oct. 22nd 1670
& sent to Bettisfield

halfe an Ounce of Dutches Gaetane cost 1 sh. 6d.
halfe an ounce of Colossus cost 1 sh. 6d.
A quarter of an ounce of Sermonettana cost 1 sh. 6d.
3 rootes of Felicite cost 1 sh. 6d.
3 rootes of Gratieuse de Paris cost a shill.
3 rootes of Superbe de France cost 1 sh.
4 rootes of Bizarre de France cost 1 sh.
Halfe an Ounce of Triumfantes cost 3 sh.
A quarter of an ounce of St Vero cost 2 sh.
A quarter of an ounce of the Great Blew of Africa cost 1 sh. 6d.
4 rootes of Henkyn de Ruyter cost 1 sh. 4d.
3 rootes, being $\frac{1}{4}$ ounce of Mirabelles cost 1 sh. 6d.
3 rootes of Gyant Golias cost 2 shill.
4 rootes of Supreme cost 1 shill.
1 roote of Bella Ceba cost 1 sh. 6d.
3 small rootes of Bride of Zealand cost 2 sh.
One ounce of Rebecca starrs cost 6d.
3 small rootes of Belle Rosée cost 1 sh. 6d.
3 rootes of Cardinall cost 1 sh. 6d.

These were all set under the South pale in the orchard at Bettisfield Nov. 1670.

Anemones bought of George Ricketts, Oct. 22nd 1670
& sent downe presently to Bettisfield

4 small rootes of Albigeoise
3 rootes of Blindenburg
2 rootes of Extravagant
2 good rootes of Ricketts owne Violett Imperiall cost 8 sh.

These were set with Le Pere's emmonyes under the South pale in the orchard.

Beares eares from Ricketts sent to Bettisfield
from Lond. Oct. 1670

1. The sable Auricular
2. the Dowble
3. a Stript Leathercoat (this died the first yeare)
4. A Scarlet
5. a purple & white (it proved another sort)
6. An Olave

These were of his best Auriculars, and were all set in potts at Bettisf. this wynter. 1670. The dowble cost 4 sh. the roote, the rest 1 sh. the roote apiece.

Gilliflowers bought of Ricketts, Octob. 1670, *& sent to Bettisf.*
(set in the full earth in the pheasant garden)

Belle Gentoise, Cleopatra, Augustina, White speckled of Harlem, Ulisses, Eagle Royall, Duke of Burgundy, Dutches of Brabant, Alliance Imperiall, Virgin of England.

These ten were all set in the ground in the pheasant garden, and cost 1 sh. the roote.

Gilliflowers bought of Le Pere, Oct. 1670, *and sent to Bettisfield*

Crowne of England, purple & white, very great flower.
Royall Soveraigne, scarlett & white.
Leckerbett, cr. & wh.

Prince Henry, deepe scarlett & white.
Marble stone, cr. & wh.
Andronicus, purp. & wh.
Adolphus, cr. & wh.
Dutches of Brabant, scarlett and white.
Browne purple, purp. & wh.
Golden Peace, sc. & wh.
These two last Gilliflowers died before Christmas, the rest were all sett in potts. They all cost 1 sh. the roote.

[They all died the second yeare except Dutches of Brabant, Andronicus, Royall Soveraigne & Adolphus.]

My largest best Beares Eares, which grew at Bettisfield in the Spring 1661

Collins Leathercoate, at first blowing paler and more yellowish haire color, afterwards more reddish. The eye is pale yellow, but whitish after. Early flower, good head.
Lookers Leathercoate, light yellow haire color, the flowers sett very thicke together. Much lighter than Collins', good white eye, a very great head, lasts long in flower, large mealy leafe.
Turners Leathercoate, a darker haire color than Lockers, but not soe red as Collins'. [Early this yeare, 1662.]
De Mowes leathercoate, bare not. (quare what t'is?)
The Yeoman of Kent, a strong plant, it beares a great head of faire open flowers of a kind of olive color, somthing like Rose's olive, but this is yellower & not soe deepe. The eye is first white, but turns pale yellow quickly. It bare late with mee this yeare, 1661.
My violett, with a pure white eye, only one roote, it blew this yeare, 1662, the earliest of all the good kinds, [early also 1663,] great head of flowers.
My light Murrey, with a broad white eye, it beares somtimes 30 flowers on a stalke. It blowes with the first, and continues with the last that blowes.

Royall Orenge, a durty orenge, with a yellowish eye, but a good head and great bearer, good for seed of the middle season.
Walkers Sandycoate, alias Gooseberry, very large flower of a sand color, with a large lemmon color eye.
Walkers Livercolor, with a lemmon color eye, whitish at first, early flower, very large, reasonable great head, [early 1663.]
Walkers Dearecolor, large flower, lemmon eye, early.
My Dove color, with a pale yellow eye, a very good flower. Blowes early, and lasts long blowing, a strong high stalke with a handsome head, standing round and orderly. Great long deepe greene leafe.
My Cinnamon, with a yellowish glosse, the eye white at first but weares yellow, the stalke long, and the head indifferent but the flowers stand more close together.

My middle siz'd Beares eares that blew at Bettisfield in Aprill 1661

1. Buffe yellow, with an ill eye, very early flower.
2. Gold yellow, with a very white eye, late flower.
3. Very pale yellow, with a reasonable eye, wh. weares out. Middle seas.
4. Very pale Dove color, with an ill eye. [Very early, 1662.] An ill flower, short stalkes, many on a head.
5. Small browne purple with a good white eye, great bearer and reasonable early.
6. Blacke Emperour, a deeper, blacker purple than the last, very white eye, and opens wide this yeare. Hardy.
7. Red Bull, a good shining cherry red, with a very white eye, reasonable strong stalke & good head. Very late.
8. Blacke purple with a durty yellow eye. Early.
9. Fire du feu, orenge and yellow towards the edges. [Early 1663.]
10. Purple and yellow stript, greene sad leafe, middle season.

11. Purple and white striped.
12. Roses olive, it never bare a great head with mee, neither did the flowers open well, but stood curl'd up still. The color is a very good deepe olive, sadder than ye Yeoman of Kent, and the eye white at first, but quickly changes. It flower'd late this yeare, 1661.
13. Virgins gift, it blew late this yeare, a bright purple pansy color, with a very white eye, and small head.
14. Purple Francois, late.
15. Faire Francis, late.

My least flower'd Beares eares that blew at Bettisfield Aprill 1661

1. *Prince of Orenge*, with a white eye that weares away, early flower.
2. *Crimson velvet*, a shining red with a white eye wearing away. Late.
3. *Stocke gilliflower*, of the color of the ordinary red stocke gilliflower, flowers very late.

My Primroses that blew at Bettisfield in the Spring, '60 & '61

The common yellow or creame color.
The pure white.
A faded dusty pale grideline.
A sand color or reddish grideline.
A blewish murrey.
A deepe shining red, the most esteem'd of all, it flowers not till the end of March, the rest begin to flower in Jan.
The greene primrose, hose in hose.
The dowble creame color.

All the primroses have yellow starry five-pointed eyes.

My Cowslips, Spring 1660 *and* 1661

(the spring very wett and cold, the wynter open & warme, no frost or snow)

1. The common yellow, hose in hose, late flower.
2. A pale dusty faded grideline, very early flower, reasonable large.
3. A murrey which comes out first pale red, and turnes deeper red, & at last blewish. No hose in hose. Very early & lasts long.
4. A fine bright shining pale reddish grideline, reasonable faire flower with a broad yellow eye. Late. [Early this yeare, 1662.]
5. A deeper red shining grideline, with a very large flower, as bigg as a primrose, with a very faire yellow eye. Great head & lasts long, hose in hose.
6. Another deeper but duller red, and as large as the former, the yellow eye dull. No hose in hose.
7. The Orenge cowslip, with flowers no bigger than the ordinary field cowslip. It flowers late.
8. The dowble yellow, t'is the common field cowslip very dowble, comes late in the beginning of May.
9. The greene feather'd cowslip in Aprill.
10. The single yellow almost white, with many greene small leaves under and about the flower. Aprill.
11. The greene cowslip, had from Blackley, with leaves under the flowers, like the greene primrose. Blew at Bettisf. March 1663.

INDEX

N

INDEX

Compiled by IVY ELSTOB

Main references are indicated by italic figures
Capitals indicate headings of Sections

List of Subscribers to the 1991 Edition

Barbara Abbs	Lewes	
Dr M. Addyman	Pickering	
Miss Vera Ackroyd	Leeds	
Derek Adlam	Welbeck	
Mr T. Allott	Amersham	
Amgueddfa Genedlaethol Cymru	Caerdydd	
Mr & Mrs T. M. Amos	Merseyside	
John Anthony	Lincoln	
Jackie Ashurst	London	
Pauline M. Atkins	Kirkby Stephen	6
Mrs I. Baish	Bristol	
Rosa Baker	Rhosesmor	2
Jean Balderson	Bangor-on-Dee	
Mrs Carole Baldwin	Macclesfield	
David Baldwin	Altrincham	
N. E. Balston	Devizes	
Mrs J. Banks	Bettisfield	2
Mrs Lesley Barker	Hawarden	
Mrs J. H. Barlow	Hanmer	
Iann Barron	Barrow Gurney	
Bath Preservation Trust	Bath	
Ms R. Batsvik	Oxford	
Mrs R. M. Bebb	Broughton Stockbridge	
Joan Beddoe	Ellsmere	
Captn T. M. Bell	St Asaph	
Steve Bennett	Caerwys	
Mrs J. H. Benson	Chiswick	
Miss S. H. Benson	Chiswick	
James Bentley	Buckley	
Mary Bland	Evenjobb	10
Caroline Boisset-Carter	Isley Walton Manor	
Ann Bonar	Folkestone	
J. R. E. Borrow	Culcheth	
Miss P. Boughton	Midhurst	
Mrs P. M. Bowen	Melton	
George Breeze	Cheltenham	
Mrs A. M. Brodribb	Oxford	
Jennifer Brown	Leeds	
S. N. R. & S. E. Brunt	Halkyn	
Mrs Bumford	Aberdyfi	
Mrs J. K. Burt	Newton Bromswold	
John S. Butler	Accrington	
Anna Buxton	Edinburgh	10
Mrs M. Campbell-Culver	Cremyll	
Miss J. Cann	Biggar	
Ianthe Carswell	London	2
Mr J. Caswell	Upton	
Dr B. Charnley	Defynnog	
Mrs B. Clark	Isle of Man	
E. D. Clarke	London	

Mrs E. L. Clarke	Yaxham	
Patricia Cleveland-Peck	East Grinstead	
C. H. Coates	Moddershall	
Carol Collis	Oban	
J. F. I. Comins	Birlingham	
Mrs A. Cowell	Hatfield Peverel	2
Mrs J. Crosby	Stanhope	
Mrs C. E. Cross	Priston	
Dr D. R. Davies	Tilstock	
E. R. Ll. Davies	Gwernymynydd	
Edith Davies	Wrexham	2
John Davies	Manchester	
Thelma Davies	Tremeirchion	
Mrs R. Davies-Colley	Chester	
Brian Davis	Newbury	
Julia Finette Davis	Pennsylvania	
Department of Architecture Planning and Estates	Mold	
Mrs M. Christina De Trute	Tenterden	
Mrs Dingwall	Bishop Auckland	
Mrs Rosemary Dingwall	Lyford	
S. M. Diviney	London	
Hugh Dixon	Morpeth	
A. K. Wolley Dod	Malpas	
Thomas Parry Dodd	Flint	
S. Doncaster	Whaley Bridge	2
Mrs S. P. Douglas	Handforth	
L. J. Drake	Cambridge	
Sir Dudley & Lady Dudley-Smith	Warwickshire	
Ruth Duthie	Oxford	
Ann Edwards	Nercwys	
Paul Edwards	Leamington Spa	
M. Elam	Kingston upon Thames	
Marilyn A. Elm	Thirsk	
Christopher J. Elvy	Hockworthy	
D. Morgan Evans	Surbiton	
Mrs H. Evans	London	
Lindsay Evans	Wrexham	2
M. E. Evans	Denbigh	
Mr R. Paul Evans	Ruthin	
Daphne Everett	Bringsty	
J. Fearnley-Whittingstall	Wotton Under Edge	
Mrs J. M. Feisenberger	London	
James Fenton	Oxford	
Mrs M. B. Field	London	
Mrs N. R. Fisher	Bath	
A. P. Fletcher	Royston	
Edward C. Foreman	Evancoyd	2
Miss H. A. Formby	Ysceifiog	
Mr E. Forster	Neston	
Dr Paul G. M. Foster	Chichester	
Beti & Ben Price Francis	Llanbedr D. C.	
Michael Franklin	Nunnington	

S. Fraser	Partridge Green	
Miss Margaret D. Fuller	Reading	
Miss A. Furber	Rhos	
Lt Col S. J. Furness	Eyemouth	
Mr A. M. Furse	Liverpool	
Mrs A. W. Furse	Mold	11
Miss J. E. Furse	Leeds	
Mr P. M. Furse	London	
Mrs R. C. Furse	London	
Mrs W. D. Furse	Birmingham	
Dr R. Gaind	Bearstead	4
Lt Col R. Gayre	Inverary	
Mrs L. Gee	Lampeter	
P. R. Giffard	Wolverhampton	
A. Glyde	Eastrop	
Philip C. Godsal	Whitchurch	2
Peter Goodchild	York	
K. M. Goodway	Keele	
Daphne Goodwin	Ruthin	2
R. B. Gorer	Heathfield	
Caroline Gould	Walton	
Miss L. F. Gould	Onslow Village	
Miss M. E. Graham	Ruthin	
Miss J. A. Green	Stedham	
Robert James Gresley	Higher Kinnerton	
J. Griffith	Denbigh	
Mrs J. G. Griffith	Trefnant	3
Owen C. Griffith	Kingswinford	
Cllr. J. H. Griffiths	Rhyl	
H. Groenewald	Mold	
Dorothy Guest	Bangor-on-Dee	
Guille-Alles Library	Guernsey	
D. T. C. Hanbury	Turvey	
Mr D. Hance	Chelmsford	
D. R. Harris	Cottingham	
Mrs J. M. Harry	Louth	
Carole Harvey	Richmond	
Mrs Ruth Hayden	Bath	
Jean M. Hemming	Crugybar	
Captain A. J. C. Hildyard DL	Barrow on Humber	
P. Hine	Whitchurch	
Penelope Hobhouse	Yeovil	
Peter Holden Architects	Pembroke	
Dr T. D. S. Holliday	Chester	2
Keith A. Honess	Winchester	
Mr N. Horton	Chesterfield	
Hugh Owen Library, University of Wales	Aberystwyth	
Mrs B. M. Hughes	Mold	
D. R. Hughes	Buckley	
Einion Hughes	Y Rhyl	
Vernon Hughes	Abergele	
John Dixon Hunt	Bicester	

Ms Sue Illman	Cheltenham	
C. K. Jackson-Houlston	Wolverhampton	
G. Jackson-Stops	London	
Chris James	Isle of Mull	2
Jon James	Rhydymwyn	
Fiona Jamieson	Edinburgh	
Mr & Mrs N. Jee	Guernsey	
Simon Johnson	Middle Chinnock	
Miss B. Trevor Jones	Hope	
D. Ffoulkes Jones	Treuddyn	
E. W. Jones MA, PhD	Oxford	
Gareth Charles Jones	Wrexham	
Grace Jones	Treuddyn	
Mr K. W. Jones	Rossett	
M. Jones	Wrexham	
Nia Wyn Jones	Bwcle	
M. C. Jones-Mortimer	Mold	6
Dr S. L. Jury	Reading	
Mary Keen	Reading	
Mr M. P. Kemp	Guildford	
Mrs Anne Kenrick	Edgbaston	
A. R. Killick	Worcester Park	
Dr Diana Kingham	Harpenden	
J. A. H. Kingswell	Wallington	
Mrs Margaret Kinnear	Edinburgh	
The Landscape Practice	Northallerton	
Judy & Winston Lea	Treuddyn	
The Leeds Library	Leeds	
Hazel Le Rougetel	Bramshott	
Michael Leslie	Sheffield	2
Ms B. J. Lewis	Leigh	
J. B. Lewis	Chester	
The Earl of Lindsay	Fife	
P. A. B. Llewellyn	Tal-y-Bont, Bangor	2
A. Wyn Lloyd	Llanfair D. C.	
Daniel Lloyd	Chertsey	
Thomas Lloyd	Kilgetty	
E. L. Lloyd-Hughes	Birmingham	
Col T. D. Lloyd-Jones	Forfar	
Llyfrgell Genedlaethol Cymru	Aberystwyth	2
F. P. Lole	Manchester	
W. A. Lord	Cheltenham	
Dr McCarter	Hanmer	
Charis Imogen McCarter	Westlake	
Miss A. M. McCosh	London	
Mrs D. J. McCosh	London	
Mrs E. H. McCosh	Biggar	2
Dr K. L. MacGregor	Dundee	
Dawn MacLeod	Cockburnspath	
R. H. D. MacNair	Pennal	
Jonathan Marsden	Denbigh	2
Mrs George Marshall	London	

Lucy Marson	Wickham	
Mrs Caryl Mason	Gwernymynydd	
Mrs E. B. Matthews	Manchester	
Mrs J. Matthews	Brampton	
Francis Menotti	Gifford	
Mrs P. A. Meyrick	Oakmere	
H. T. Moggridge	Lechlade	
Ivan Molyneux	Abergele	2
Dr M. L. Moncrieff	Leominster	
Ms Alex Monro	London	
Patricia Moore	Penarth	
Patricia M. Moran	London	
Anne Morris	Swansea	
Mrs E. Morris	Market Drayton	
Miss S. Morris	Cirencester	
Barbara Morton	London	
Dr Timothy Mowl	Bristol	
Keiran Murray	Oswestry	
Mrs K. Myers	London	
National Trust for Scotland	Edinburgh	
M. Nelson	Bournemouth	
Mrs Ann Noltie	Dundee	
D. S. Nunn	Sutton	
Mrs D. Nutting	Newport Pagnell	
Mrs S. O'Neill	Bath	
Mrs F. K. Oglethorpe	Woking	
John Owen	Conwy	
William Pack	Minster Lovell	
A. J. Palmer	Norwich	
Mark Paterson	Wivenhoe	2
Patricia Payne	Minehead	
Mary Perry	Norbury	10
J. L. Phibbs	Bath	
J. Phillips	Sutton	
Mr W. Pollintiner	Whitford	
Derrick Pratt	Welsh Frankton	
Geoffrey F. O. D. Pratt	Ellesmere	
Mr J. M. Prest	Wheatley	
Dr J. Stainton Price	Padstow	
Mrs L. S. Price	Stanmore	
P. M. C. Probert	Llanarmon yn Ial	
The Countess of Radnor	Salisbury	2
Frederick Rapsey	Haughley Green	5
Timothy Raylor	Hathersage	
Mr J. D. Rea FLS	London	
Albert F. Rice	Northampton	
Anne Richards	Hereford	
Mrs S. A. Richards	Cambridge	
C. I. Richmond-Watson	Charing	
The Hon Mrs Roberts	Windsor	
H. M. Roberts	West Auckland	
Mr J. B. M. Roberts	Portishead	

G. J. Robeson	Norwich	
Peter Q. Rose	Castle Cary	
Valerie & Alex Rouse	Hanmer	
Mr & Mrs W. R. Rowley	Mold	
R. W. Rutherford	Reading	2
J. P. Savidge	Aberystwyth	
E. M. Scattergood	Hope	
Julie Schofield	Shepton Mallet	
Andrew Sclater	Llandeilo	2
Simone Sekers	Dorking	
Mr A. D. Short	Gillingham	
Mrs P. Singleton	Mold	
Ian Michael Smart	Manchester	
Mr G. P. Smith	Wrexham	
Paul Smith	Ludlow	
B. Snaddon	Bath	
Mrs J. Soutter	Mold	2
Mr & Mrs G. V. Springett	Tunbridge Wells	
Mr & Mrs R. A. G. Springett	Bettisfield	
D. J. Stagg	Guernsey	
P. K. Stembridge	Bristol	
Lady Shaw Stewart	Inverkip	
H. J. M. Stratton	Ottershaw	
W. B. Sullivan	Rugeley	
Tatton Park	Knutsford	
Dr Hilary A. Taylor	Nottingham	
John Taylor	Llanbedr D. C.	
Mrs P. Taylor	Chester	
H. M. Temple-Richards	Fakenham	
E. Tennant	Newcastleton	
Dr C. Thacker	Midgham Green	
Mrs Diane Thomas	Northop Hall	
Hilli Thompson	Ipswich	
M. Thompson	Ewloe Green	
Mrs S. Thorneycroft	Monmouth	
Benjamin Tindall	Edinburgh	
Stephen J. Torode FLS	Cardiff	2
P. Travers	Rhos-on-Sea	
Michael Tree	Llangollen	
Anne Marie Tremlett	Oxford	
Mrs G. E. Trefor-Williams	Pentre Halkyn	
R. C. Turner	Penarth	
Mrs Joyce Turton	Caergwrle	
Sir Harry & Lady Tuzo	Fakenham	
Hon Lloyd Tyrell-Kenyon	Whitchurch	2
W. T. C. Walker	Leeds	
N. A. Walmsley	Trefor	
Mrs K. E. Walsh	Pencader	
Miss D. Waterworth	Cadole	
Mr J. G. Waterworth	Cadole	
Mrs M. Watson	Market Harborough	
Robin Whalley	Llanfrynach	

Mrs E. Wheeler	Crymych	
D. Whitehead	Hereford	
Miss R. Whittingham	Mold	
Mrs Elisabeth Whittle	Usk	
Walter Wilde	Stourport on Severn	
Mrs K. Wilkinson	Ruabon	
Roger Wilkinson	Malpas	
Mrs H. P. M. Williams	Brynford	
J. R. Williams	Denbigh	
Selwyn Williams	Old Colwyn	
Mrs E. Wilson	Wittersham	
M. Witton-Davies	Mold	2
E. H. Wood	Rhuddlan	
Jan Woudstra	London	
Wrexham Maelor Museum Service	Wrexham	
A. G. L. Wright	London	
Dr Margaret Wright	Drayton Parslow	
C. P. Younie	London	